Crime Scene Detective
ARSON

Karen K. Schulz

Illustrated by Mike Eustis & David Parker

Prufrock Press Inc.

Copyright ©2007 Prufrock Press Inc.

Edited by Lacy Elwood
Editorial Assistant: Kate Sepanski
Illustrated by Mike Eustis & David Parker
Production Design by Marjorie Parker

ISBN-13: 978-1-59363-234-2
ISBN-10: 1-59363-234-7

The purchase of this book entitles the buyer to reproduce student activity pages for classroom use only. Other use requires written permission of publisher. All rights reserved.

At the time of this book's publication, all facts and figures cited are the most current available; all telephone numbers, addresses, and Web site URLs are accurate and active; all publications, organizations, Web sites, and other resources exist as described in this book; and all have been verified. The authors and Prufrock Press make no warranty or guarantee concerning the information and materials given out by organizations or content found at Web sites, and we are not responsible for any changes that occur after this book's publication. If you find an error or believe that a resource listed here is not as described, please contact Prufrock Press.

Prufrock Press Inc.
P.O. Box 8813
Waco, TX 76714-8813
Phone: (800) 998-2208
Fax: (800) 240-0333
http://www.prufrock.com

Contents

Dedication

This book is dedicated to Jim, Taylor, and Matthew, who always keep me smiling, and to Aunt Susie Caudle, who is an inspiration to all who know her.

Acknowledgements

As a gifted education teacher, I am always looking for ways to challenge my students. Criminal investigations and solving mysteries are exciting topics that model real-world situations. The first *Crime Scene Detective* book was published in 2003. Over the years I have created additional storylines to use with this unit. *Crime Scene Detective: Arson* contains six new storylines and additional student materials. These storylines can be used exclusively or can be combined with the storylines from the original *Crime Scene Detective*.

A special thanks goes out to arson investigator John Raines, his new canine partner, Blaze, and to polygraph examiner Randy Combs, both with the St. Louis County Police Department. Their continuing commitment to visit my classroom and share their knowledge with my students is greatly appreciated.

Thanks also to the staff members at Wildwood Middle School for their participation in this simulation. I couldn't ask for a better group of suspects and witnesses.

Finally, I must thank my husband, Jim, and children, Taylor and Matthew, for letting me bounce ideas off of them, for giving me suggestions, and for their continued support. It doesn't get any better than this.

Teacher's Guide

Introduction

A variety of crimes, including robberies, arson, counterfeiting, computer fraud, and murder, are committed each day. Advances in science have allowed scientists to gather and analyze evidence from even the most minute traces. This is called *forensic science*.

Students are often taught skills such as the scientific method, scientific research, critical thinking, making observations, analyzing facts, and drawing conclusions in isolation. Studying forensic science allows students to practice these skills and see theories put into practice by using circumstances that model real-life events. Students also will explore a variety of career opportunities.

Unit Description

This unit is divided into three main parts:
- In Part I, students learn general information about criminal investigations. Topics include police procedures at a crime scene, evidence collection, the Locard principle, the scientific method, and forensic science careers. The teacher teaches these lessons.
- In Part II, students research various types of evidence (hair, odontology, anthropology, fingerprints, ballistics, etc.), create a lesson, and teach it to the class.
- In Part III, students apply the information they have learned by participating in a schoolwide crime scene investigation. A simulation is provided that involves a fire in the school library media center. The suspects are teachers and other staff members in the school. To stage this simulation you will need the cooperation of staff members. This is an experience that both students and teachers alike enjoy.

Guest speakers may be invited to speak any time during the unit. Guest speakers may include an FBI agent, fingerprinting expert, ballistics expert, arson investigator, detective, forensic lab specialist, Secret Service agent, polygraph examiner, entomologist, or a medical examiner. Throughout this unit, students may also participate in a variety of forensic science experiments.

Upon completing this unit, you may want to have your students conduct a mock trial in which the accused from the simulation is placed on trial. A mock trial is a great way to show students the complete process of the criminal justice system, beginning with a crime and ending with a trial. However, you may also choose to have students present their accused suspect to you via an oral or written report.

In addition to the simulation that is provided, there are instructions in Appendix A (see pp. 87–91) for writing your own simulation. If you do not wish to use the simulation provided, you can create a scenario that is custom tailored to your school. You may also use a combination of the storylines provided and ones that you write yourself.

Standards and Learning Objectives

By participating in this unit, the learner will:
- study and apply the scientific method as it relates to a criminal investigation;
- recognize the role science plays in a criminal investigation;
- collect data by observing, measuring, and questioning;
- distinguish between relevant and irrelevant information;
- draw inferences and conclusions based on observations, facts, and collected data;
- recognize whether evidence is consistent with a proposed explanation;
- plan and implement investigative procedures including asking questions and formulating testable hypotheses;
- apply appropriate interview techniques including preparing and asking relevant questions, making notes of responses, responding effectively to questions and comments, compiling and reporting responses, and evaluating the effectiveness of the interview;
- analyze and interpret information to construct reasonable explanations from direct and indirect evidence using logical thinking;
- analyze, review, and critique scientific explanations, including hypotheses and theories, as to their strengths and weaknesses using scientific evidence and information;
- communicate and justify the logical connections among hypotheses, science concepts, tests conducted, and conclusions drawn from scientific evidence;
- communicate the steps and results from an investigation in written reports and oral presentations; and
- become aware of careers associated with forensic science, law enforcement, and criminal justice.

Time Requirements

This unit was designed to be a semester-long course. This includes an optional mock trial, visits by a variety of guest speakers, and completion of forensic science experiments. By compacting and tailoring the unit to fit each unique learning situation, it could be taught in less time.

Grade Levels

This forensic science unit was developed for a middle school gifted education class. By adjusting the individual lessons and project requirements this unit easily could be used with grades 4–12.

Assessment

Students are assessed in a variety of ways. In Part I of the unit, students are given a quiz over the note-taking materials covered in the teacher's lectures. Students are also given a written assignment covering the career awareness topics discussed in the second lesson. In Part II, students may be graded on the completion of each component of the lesson they are creating (note taking, outline, note sheet, works consulted, etc.) and then graded on the evidence lesson they teach to the class. In the simulation section of the unit, students are graded on the detective reports they write. Multiple reports throughout the duration of the simulation may be required. The teacher may also choose to grade students on the notes they take during their interviews of suspects and witnesses. At the conclusion of the investigation, students may be asked to write a final report describing who is being charged with the crime and justifying their decision with specific facts from the investigation.

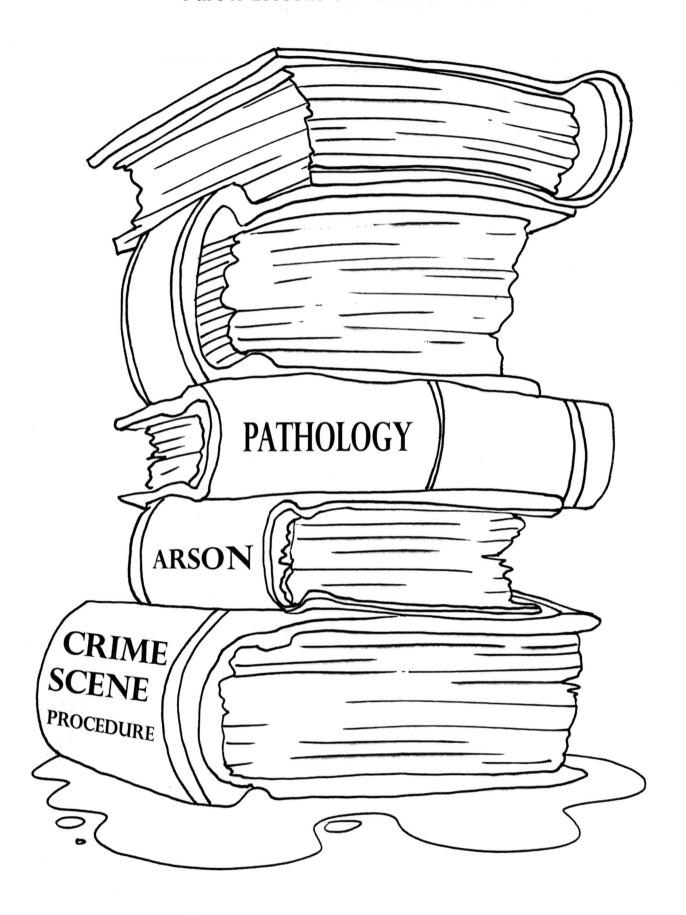

Lesson 1: Criminal Investigations

Materials

- Criminal Investigations: Topics of Discussion information sheets (see pp. 10–11)
- Criminal Investigations Student Note-Taking Sheet (optional; see pp. 12–14)
- Overhead transparencies or multimedia presentation (optional)

Procedures

- Introduce students to basic information on criminal investigations by discussing the following:
  - definition of forensic science,
  - Locard's principle,
  - types of evidence,
  - police procedures at a crime scene,
  - procedures for gathering evidence,
  - crime lab procedures,
  - the scientific method.
- You can use the information and graphics on pp. 10–11 to make transparencies or create a multimedia slideshow presentation. Using this information as an outline, elaborate on each topic as you discuss the information with your students.
- You also may have students take notes on this presentation using the included note sheet on pp. 12–14.

Criminal Investigations: Topics of Discussion

Forensic Science

Forensic science is the scientific examination of evidence in a criminal investigation.

Locard's Principle

This principle was developed in 1910 by Edmond Locard. It states that criminals always take a trace of something with them and leave a trace of something behind at the scene of the crime.

Police Procedures at the Crime Scene

There are several things that police routinely do at a crime scene. The typical procedures are (listed in the order they are performed):
1. Check the victim.
2. Secure the area.
3. Document the area.
    a. Photograph, sketch, or videotape the crime scene.
    b. Take measurements.
4. Thoroughly search for and collect evidence.
5. Interview any witness(es).

Evidence

Evidence is anything that helps prove the guilt or innocence of a person suspected of a crime. There are two types of evidence—direct and circumstantial.

Direct Evidence

Direct evidence is evidence that proves the fact without a doubt. This includes having an eyewitness to the crime or having a videotape showing the crime being committed.

Circumstantial Evidence

Circumstantial evidence is sometimes called indirect evidence. This type of evidence provides supporting facts to establish the truth through indirect means.

For instance, if the suspect recently bought the same type of poison or owns the same type of gun involved in the crime, that is considered circumstantial evidence. Even if a suspect's fingerprints are found at the scene of the crime, it is still circumstantial. Prints alone don't prove a suspect committed the crime.

© Prufrock Press Inc. • *Crime Scene Detective: Arson*
This page may be photocopied or reproduced with permission for student use.

Collecting Evidence

When police acquire evidence at a crime scene, they follow certain procedures to make sure the evidence is preserved and documented. Police must be able to prove that the evidence never left their possession. They typically follow these steps:

- Each possible piece of evidence collected is put in its own container. The container is labeled and sealed.
- The label indicates where and when it was found and is initialed by the officer who found it.
- The evidence is then sent to the crime or forensic lab.

At the Forensic Lab

Once the evidence is received at the forensic lab, the following procedures are taken:

- Each object is listed in the evidence register.
- Evidence is kept in a locked room. Only authorized people can examine it.
- An exact record is kept of each person who has handled the evidence.
- Evidence is examined by people who are specially trained to analyze and interpret it.

Scientific Method

When detectives are trying to solve a crime, they use the scientific method. Scientists commonly use this method to observe what is happening and to test various explanations. It consists of these five steps (in this order):

1. Gather as much evidence as possible.
2. Study all the available evidence.
3. Look for errors or inconsistencies.
4. Form a hypothesis or explanation.
5. Test the hypothesis in all possible ways.

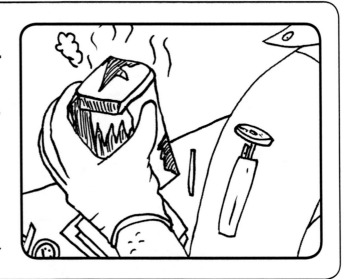

Name:_____ Date:_____

Criminal Investigations
Student Note-Taking Sheet

Directions: Fill in the blanks as each criminal investigation topic is discussed.

Forensic Science

Forensic science is the _____ examination

of _____ in a _____ investigation.

Locard's Principle

This principle was developed in _____ by _____. It

states that criminals always _____ of something with them and

_____ of something behind at the scene of the crime.

Police Procedures at the Crime Scene

There are several things that police routinely do at a crime scene. The typical

procedures are (listed in the order they are performed):

1. _____.

2. _____.

3. _____.
   a. Photograph, sketch, or videotape the crime scene.
   b. Take measurements.

4. Thoroughly _____ for and

   _____ evidence.

5. _____ any witness(es).

Evidence

Evidence is anything that helps prove the _____ or

_____ of a person suspected of a _____. There

are two types of evidence: _____ and _____.

© Prufrock Press Inc. • *Crime Scene Detective: Arson*
This page may be photocopied or reproduced with permission for student use.

Direct Evidence

_____ evidence is

evidence that _____ the

fact without a _____.

Examples include having an

_____ to the crime or a

_____ of the crime

being committed.

Circumstantial Evidence

_____ evidence is sometimes called _____

evidence. This type of evidence provides _____ facts to

establish the truth through _____ means.

    For instance, if the suspect recently bought the same type of poison or owns

the same type of gun involved in the crime, that is considered circumstantial

evidence. Even if a suspect's fingerprints are found at the scene of the crime, it is

still _____. Prints alone don't prove a suspect committed the

crime.

Collecting Evidence

When police acquire evidence at a crime scene, they follow certain procedures to

make sure the evidence is preserved and documented. Police must be able to prove

that evidence never left their possession. They typically follow these steps:

- Each possible piece of _____ collected is put in its own

_____. The container is _____

and _____.

- The label indicates _____ and _____

it was found and is _____ by the officer who found it.

- The evidence is then sent to the crime or _____ lab.

At the Forensic Lab

Once the evidence is received at the forensic lab, the following procedures are taken.

- Each _____ is listed in the evidence _____.

- _____ is kept in a _____ room.

  Only _____ people can examine it.

- An exact _____ is kept of each person who has

  _____ the evidence.

- Evidence is examined by people who are specially trained to

  _____ and _____ it.

Scientific Method

When detectives are trying to solve a crime, they use the scientific method.

Scientists commonly use this method to observe what is happening and to test

various explanations. It consists of these five steps (in this order):

1. _____ as much _____ as possible.

2. _____ all the available _____.

3. Look for _____ or _____.

4. Form a _____ or _____.

5. _____ the _____ in all possible ways.

© Prufrock Press Inc. • *Crime Scene Detective: Arson*
This page may be photocopied or reproduced with permission for student use.

Lesson 2: Forensic Science Care

Materials

- Forensic Science: It's Not Just a Career, It's an Adven.
  sheets (see pp. 16–17)
- Becoming a Forensic Scientist information sheet (see p. 1.
- Forensic Science: It's Not Just a Career, It's an Adventure! Stu.
  Taking Sheet (optional; see pp. 19–21)
- Becoming a Forensic Scientist Student Note-Taking Sheet (optiona.
  22–23)
- Forensic Science: It's Not Just a Career, It's an Adventure! Career Story
  Assignment (optional; see p. 24)
- The Field of Forensic Science Quiz for assessment (optional; see pp. 25–26)
- Overhead transparencies or multimedia presentation

Procedure

- Tell students that there are many different people who are involved in
  a criminal investigation. Consequently, there are many different career
  opportunities.
- Create a presentation entitled "Forensic Science Careers," using the printed
  copy on pp. 16–18 as a guideline. You may choose to make the pages
  into transparencies for an overhead projector or create a PowerPoint
  presentation. Discuss the various jobs that may be involved in a forensic
  laboratory. You may have students take notes on this presentation using the
  included note sheet on pp. 19–23.
- An optional homework assignment and quiz covering this information
  have been included on pp. 24–26.

...nsic Science: It's Not Just a Career, It's an Adventure!

Forensic scientists use their knowledge of science to help determine the facts and truth in both civil and criminal matters. This is a gratifying career choice for those with a love of science and a desire to see justice served.

There are a variety of careers involving different branches of science within the field of forensic science. These careers appeal to a wide variety of interests and abilities. An investigation of a crime may use any or all of the following specialists.

Odontologist

An odontologist is a dentist who applies the principles of dentistry to identify human remains and bite marks.

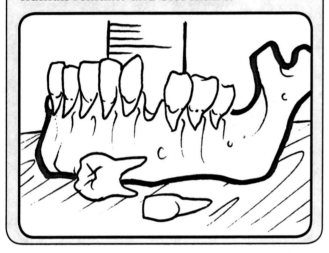

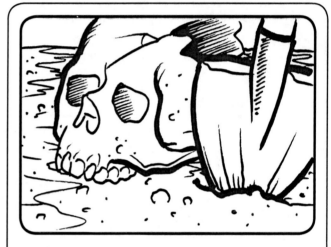

Forensic Anthropologist

A forensic anthropologist identifies skeletal remains and determines sex, age, race, or marks of trauma.

Pathologist

A pathologist is a medical doctor who determines cause of death by performing an autopsy.

Forensic Engineer

A forensic engineer applies engineering concepts in legal situations (for instance, accident reconstruction or failure analysis).

© Prufrock Press Inc. • *Crime Scene Detective: Arson*
This page may be photocopied or reproduced with permission for student use.

Ballistic Analyst

A ballistic analyst examines guns and ammunition and interprets gunshot wounds or gunshot marks and residue.

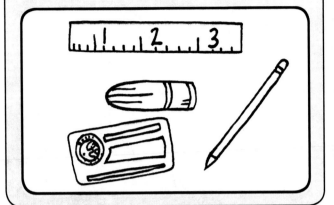

Psychiatrist

A psychiatrist analyzes human behavior to determine what motivates a criminal, determines his or her competence, and assesses the mental state of the accused.

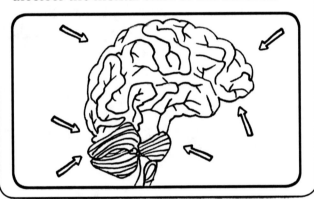

Toxicologist

A toxicologist's specialty is poisons. A toxicologist determines if drugs or other chemicals (poisons) contributed to the cause of death or were present in a crime.

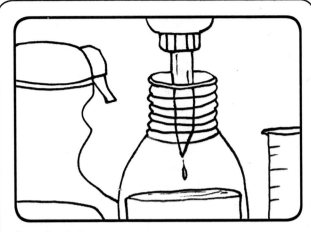

Serologist

A serologist identifies and examines blood and other bodily fluids.

Document Examiner

A document examiner analyzes written documents. He may study handwriting, typewriting, paper, ink, and any other features of documents.

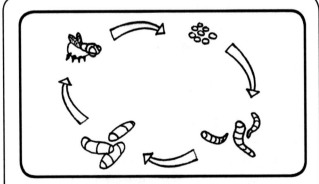

Forensic Entomologist

An entomologist studies the life cycles of insects to help determine the approximate time of death of a victim in a murder investigation.

Becoming a Forensic Scientist

Educational requirements will vary depending on specific fields of interest. A bachelor's degree is a minimum requirement for most jobs. This degree may be in chemistry, biology, physics, or anthropology. A medical degree may be necessary for some jobs.

In addition to formal training, other requirements may include coursework in science and math, continuing education to keep current on new procedures, and board certification in the desired area of expertise.

Special Skills

Being a successful forensic scientist involves more than just getting a degree. Certain skills are a must. These include:

- good eyesight and keen observation skills,
- curiosity and imagination,
- ability and patience to work with details,
- integrity,
- being objective and free from bias and prejudice, and
- ability to keep accurate records.

A forensic scientist may be called to testify in court, so he or she must also be skilled in public speaking, data management, and scientific writing.

The Workplace

Forensic scientists may work in a variety of places for different agencies. They can work in any of these capacities or workplaces:

- for local, state, or federal government;
- for a laboratory that analyzes different types of evidence;
- as an independent consultant;
- in a hospital, office, or university;
- in the morgue or medical examiner's office; and
- at the crime scene.

© Prufrock Press Inc. • *Crime Scene Detective: Arson*
This page may be photocopied or reproduced with permission for student use.

Forensic Science: It's Not Just a Career, It's an Adventure!
Student Note-Taking Sheet

Directions: Fill in the blanks as each topic is discussed.

Forensic scientists use their knowledge of

_____ to help determine the

_____ and _____

in both _____ and

_____ matters. This is a gratifying

career choice for those with a love of science and a

desire to see justice served.

    There are a variety of careers involving different

branches of science within the field of forensic science.

Theses careers appeal to a wide variety of interests and

abilities. An investigation of a crime may use any or all of

the following specialists.

Odontologist

An odontologist is a _____ who applies the principles of

dentistry to _____ human remains and _____

_____.

Forensic Anthropologist

A forensic anthropologist identifies _____ remains and

determines sex, _____, race, or marks of _____.

Pathologist

A pathologist is a medical doctor who determines _____ of

_____ by performing an _____.

© Prufrock Press Inc. • *Crime Scene Detective: Arson*
This page may be photocopied or reproduced with permission for student use.

Forensic Engineer

A forensic engineer applies _____ concepts in

_____ situations (for instance, _____

reconstruction or _____ analysis).

Ballistic Analyst

A ballistic analyst examines _____ and _____

and interprets gunshot _____ or gunshot

_____ and _____.

Serologist

A serologist _____ and examines _____ and

other bodily _____.

Psychiatrist

A psychiatrist analyzes _____ behavior to determine what

_____ a criminal, determines his or her _____,

and assesses the _____ state of the accused.

Document Examiner

A document examiner analyzes _____ documents. He may

study _____, typewriting, _____, ink, and any

other _____ of

documents.

© Prufrock Press Inc. • *Crime Scene Detective: Arson*
This page may be photocopied or reproduced with permission for student use.

Toxicologist

A toxicologist's specialty is _____. A toxicologist determines if

_____ or other _____ (poisons) contributed to

the cause of _____ or were present in a _____.

Forensic Entomologist

An entomologist studies the _____ _____ of

_____ to help determine the approximate

_____ of _____ of a victim in a murder

investigation.

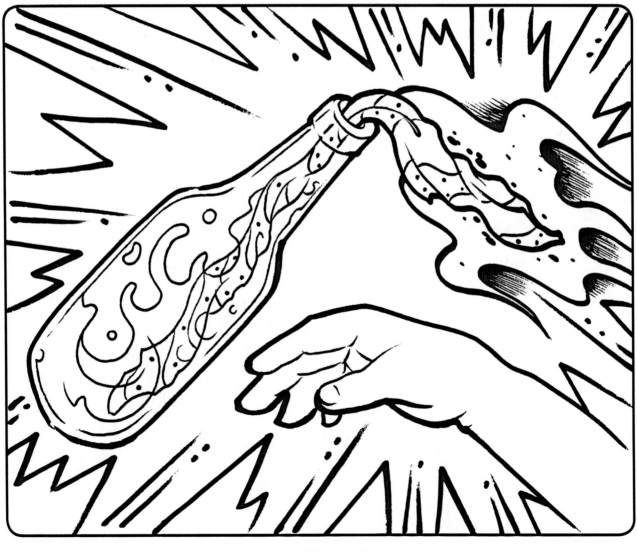

© Prufrock Press Inc. • *Crime Scene Detective: Arson*
This page may be photocopied or reproduced with permission for student use.

Name:_____ Date:_____

Becoming A Forensic Scientist
Student Note-Taking Sheet

Educational requirements will vary depending on specific fields of interest.

A _____ degree is a minimum requirement for most jobs. This

degree may be in chemistry, _____, physics,

or _____. A _____ degree may be necessary for

some jobs.

In addition to formal training, other requirements may include coursework in

_____ and _____, continuing education to

keep current on new procedures, and _____ certification in the

desired area of _____.

Special Skills

Being a successful forensic scientist involves more than just having a degree.

Certain skills are a must. These include:

- good _____ and keen _____ skills,

- _____ and imagination,

- ability and _____ to work with _____,

- integrity,

- being _____ and free from _____ and

  prejudice, and

- ability to keep _____ records.

A forensic scientist may be called to testify in court, so he or she must also be

skilled in _____ _____, data management,

and _____ writing.

© Prufrock Press Inc. • *Crime Scene Detective: Arson*
This page may be photocopied or reproduced with permission for student use.

The Workplace

Forensic scientists may work in a variety of places for different agencies. They can

work in any of these capacities or workplaces:

- for local, state, or federal _____;

- for a _____ that analyzes different types of

    _____;

- as an _____ consultant;

- in a _____, office, or university;

- in the _____ or medical examiner's office; and

- at the _____ scene.

© Prufrock Press Inc. • *Crime Scene Detective: Arson*
This page may be photocopied or reproduced with permission for student use.

Name:_____ Date:_____

Forensic Science: It's Not Just a Career, It's an Adventure!
Career Story Assignment

Have you ever wanted to be a mystery writer? Well, here's your chance! Use the information you learned from the career awareness lesson to write your own crime story. Write about *one* crime that would involve the expertise of any *three* of these careers: odontologist, forensic anthropologist, pathologist, forensic engineer, ballistic analyst, serologist, psychiatrist, document examiner, toxicologist, or forensic entomologist.

Be sure to describe the evidence that was left behind and explain which expert would handle the specific pieces of evidence. In other words, think of a situation/ crime scene that would include evidence requiring three of the above-mentioned experts to be involved. Your story should demonstrate that you understand what each of the experts does. Make sure your story is appropriate for the classroom.

Complete the chart below to help you plan your story. Write or type your final story on a separate sheet of paper as directed by your teacher.

Type of Expert (Odontologist, Toxicologist, etc.)	Job Description (What Does This Person Do?)	Possible Pieces of Evidence to Include in the Story (Bottle of Poison, Handwritten Note, etc.)

© Prufrock Press Inc. • *Crime Scene Detective: Arson*
This page may be photocopied or reproduced with permission for student use.

The Field of Forensic Science Quiz

I. **Matching.** Write the letter for the definition that best describes each career in the space next to the career's name.

_____1. forensic anthropologist

_____2. pathologist

_____3. forensic engineer

_____4. ballistic analyst

_____5. serologist

_____6. document examiner

_____7. toxicologist

_____8. odontologist

_____9. forensic entomologist

_____10. psychiatrist

A. studies the life cycles of insects to determine time of death

B. identifies skeletal remains and determines sex, age, race, or marks of trauma

C. determines if drugs or other poisons contributed to cause of death or were at the crime scene

D. applies principles of dentistry to identify unknown human remains and bite marks

E. examines guns and ammunition and interprets gunshot wounds

F. analyzes human behavior to determine what motivates a criminal

G. determines cause of death by performing an autopsy

H. identifies and examines blood and other bodily fluids

I. studies handwriting, typewriting, paper, and ink

J. applies engineering concepts in legal situations

II. **Sequence of Events.** Put these events in the correct order with 1 being the first thing you do and 5 being the last thing you would do.

Police procedures at a crime scene
_____A. Interview any witness.
_____B. Document the area (photograph, sketch, videotape, and take measurements).
_____C. Secure the area.
_____D. Check the victim.
_____E. Thoroughly search for and collect evidence.

Using the scientific method in an investigation
_____A. Test the hypothesis in all possible ways.
_____B. Gather as much evidence as possible.
_____C. Form a hypothesis or explanation.
_____D. Look for errors or inconsistencies.
_____E. Study all the available evidence.

Name:_____ Date:_____

III. **Fill in the Blank.** Fill in the blank with the word(s) that best completes the statement using the words below. You will not use all of the words.

WORD BANK:
Analysis
Circumstantial
Contact theory
Direct
Forensic science
Locard's principle
Lomand's principle
Scientific method

1. _____ is the scientific examination of evidence in a criminal investigation.

2. _____ states that "Criminals always take a trace of something with them and leave a trace of something behind at the scene of the crime."

3. Eyewitness accounts or a tape from a video camera would be examples of _____ evidence.

4. _____ evidence provides supporting facts to establish the truth through indirect means.

© Prufrock Press Inc. • *Crime Scene Detective: Arson*
This page may be photocopied or reproduced with permission for student use.

Lesson 1: Exploring Types of Evidence: Student Directed Lessons

Materials

- Exploring Types of Evidence: Student Lesson Guidelines (see p. 29)
- Exploring Types of Evidence: Planning Your Lesson sheet (see pp. 30–32)
- Exploring Types of Evidence: Grading Sheet (see p. 33)
- Posterboard, markers, and other materials for creating visual aids
- PowerPoint or other presentation software (optional)

Procedure

- Discuss different types of evidence that might be left at a crime scene. As different items are suggested, add them to a master list.
- Assign students, either individually or in small groups, a specific type of evidence to research. Possible topics may include arson; anthropology; ballistics; fingerprints; hair; fiber; DNA; odontology; tire, shoe, or tool impressions; seed, soil, or pollen; bombs or explosives; documents; handwriting samples; or blood analysis. *Note*: The students may find some topics more desirable than others. One random way of assigning topics is to write each topic on a slip of paper and have each student draw a topic. After everyone has drawn, give each student 30 seconds to trade with another student if he or she would like a different topic. At the end of the 30 seconds, students will research the topic they are holding at that time.
- After completing their research, students are to prepare a presentation to the class on their topic. You may use the assignment guidelines given on p. 29 or create your own. The guidelines given are very detailed and provide students with examples of the components of the lesson. Remember, students will be teaching others about their topics and must do so in a clear and concise manner. Giving students very detailed expectations allows for consistent lessons. You may ask students to make PowerPoint presentations if they have access to the necessary software and equipment. In lieu of the PowerPoint presentation, they may prepare lessons that make use of charts, graphs, pictures, or transparencies. Any visual aids should be large enough to be seen by everyone or easily passed around the classroom.
- You may ask each child to submit three questions, along with the answers, from his or her presentation. Using these as a pool, create a quiz for the class.
- A scoring rubric for the student presentation is included on p. 33.

Exploring Types of Evidence:
Student Lesson Guidelines

Assignment Overview

You will be assigned a specific topic concerning evidence used in a forensic investigation. Your job is to thoroughly research the topic and then prepare a lesson to teach to the class. The information in this handout, along with teacher explanations, will help you organize and prepare your lesson. (Use PowerPoint if it is available in your school.) As always, challenge yourself to do your best work and turn in a project that makes you proud.

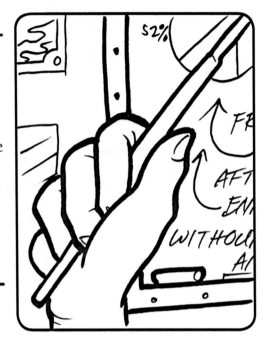

Research

Thoroughly research your topic. You need a minimum of four resources. Use at least two books and at least two Web sites, and consider contacting an expert. Remember to document your resources as you go. You may use note cards to record your findings. You will need to find at least 30 facts about your topic. Be sure to cover these topics in your research:

- a brief history or background information—include information about who, what, when, where, why, and how;
- a detailed description of the evidence (what is it?); and
- an explanation of how it is used in a criminal investigation.

Lesson Plan Format

You should follow this general format for teaching your lesson:
1. Introduction
2. Brief history or general background information
3. Specific information on what the evidence is and how it is used as in an investigation
4. An activity, experiment, or visual to enhance your presentation
5. A way to check for understanding or assessment
6. Conclusion

Planning Your Lesson

Follow the steps on the "Planning Your Lesson" sheet very carefully. Each step has a due date for when you need to have that step completed. In addition, you will be graded on how carefully you follow and complete each step.

Exploring Types of Evidence: Planning Your Lesson

Record the due date on each line below as determined by your teacher. Neatly and thoroughly complete each of the following tasks, turning in each section on the designated due date. Unless otherwise indicated, all answers should be typed or neatly written in blue or black ink on a separate sheet of paper.

Topic/Type of Evidence:

_____

Steps to Planning Your Lesson

1. Write your *essential question*: What question will your research answer? Be specific (for example, How does the polygraph instrument work and what interview techniques are used when interviewing a suspect?).

   Due date: _____

   ┌───┐
   │   **My Essential Question**   │
   │   │
   │   │
   │   │
   │   │
   │   │
   │   │
   │   │
   └───┘

2. On note cards write the *specific facts* from your research (at least 30) that you will use in your presentation.

   Due date: _____

3. *References.* Document your sources on a separate sheet of paper as you take notes. Organize this information following the guidelines established previously in class. A final copy will be typed and turned in prior to your presentation.

   Due date: _____

© Prufrock Press Inc. • *Crime Scene Detective: Arson*
This page may be photocopied or reproduced with permission for student use.

4. *Body of the lesson.* This is where all the facts about your topic are taught. Write this in outline or web form listing specific topics and supporting details in the order in which you will teach them. See the sample of a partial outline to the right.

Due date: _____

5. *Activity, experiment, or visual.* In addition to your presentation you will conduct a science experiment, plan an activity, create a visual, complete a demonstration, or do something else to enhance your presentation and encourage class participation. Check out the classroom reference books for ideas or see the teacher. The teacher must approve your ideas before you proceed with your plans. Answer these questions on a separate sheet of paper:

- Describe in detail the activity, experiment, or visual you will use in the lesson.
- How is this relevant to the topic? What skill or fact does it reinforce?
- How will this involve students in the classroom?
- What materials will you need?

Due date: _____

Sample Outline: Polygraph

I. History
   A. Invented by John Larson
   B. Invented in 1921
II. How the test works
   A. Assumes no physiological changes in telling truth
   B. Measures changes that occur during fear/stress
      1. Heart rate
      2. Perspiration
   C. Polygraph instrument measures and records changes in:
      1. Pulse rate
      2. Breathing pattern
      3. Chemical changes (perspiration)
   D. Records reactions to questions on a chart
III. Interview procedures
   A. Controlled environment
      1. Room
      2. Interviewer
      3. Subject
   B. Body language–nonverbal clues
      1. Eye contact
      2. Posture
IV. Use in a criminal investigation
   A. Voluntarily taken
   B. Used after other investigative techniques reach a dead end
   C. Hope interview produces a confession
   D. 95% effective

---

6. *Introduction to the lesson.* Write your introduction in paragraph form, using the actual wording you will use during your presentation. This is what you will say to the class as you begin your presentation. It should be able to get your classmates attention, as shown in the example below.

Due date: _____

Sample Introduction Paragraph

Have you ever told a lie? Notice how your palms get sweaty? How you get a knot in your stomach and avoid all eye contact? Polygraph examiners use these nonverbal clues along with others to determine if a suspect is lying. Today in my presentation, I will tell you about the polygraph, or lie detector instrument, and how it is used to help determine the guilt or innocence of a suspect in a criminal investigation.

---

7. *Check for understanding.* Write two or three specific questions you will ask at the end of the lesson to check to see if students understand the material (for example, What nonverbal clues does a polygraph examiner look for when interviewing a suspect? What does the polygraph instrument measure? How is the polygraph instrument used in a criminal investigation?).

Due date: _____

8. *Conclusion.* Summarize the main points and bring it to an end. Write your conclusion in paragraph form, using the exact words you will use during your lesson (see the example below).

Due date: _____

Sample Conclusion Paragraph

As you can see there are many ways of determining if a suspect is lying. Verbal and nonverbal clues play a big role and the actual polygraph instrument is only one piece of that puzzle. As a polygraph examiner once said, "The eyes are the windows to the soul."

---

9. *Note sheet.* Your classmates will be taking notes during your lesson. Make sure your ideas are presented in a way that is organized, clear, and easily understood. You must prepare a note sheet (two pages maximum) for students to use during your presentation. This note sheet must be fill-in-the-blank style, with one or two blanks (key words) per sentence. Do not have your classmates write full sentences—it takes too long. Not every sentence needs to have blanks to fill in. This sheet should include all of the main ideas on your topic. It should be written *after* you have finished working on your presentation to make sure it follows the format of the lesson. This note sheet must be turned in for approval prior to the presentation of the lesson. Follow the format of the note sheet you completed while taking notes on Lessons 1 and 2.

© Prufrock Press Inc. • *Crime Scene Detective: Arson*
This page may be photocopied or reproduced with permission for student use.

Name:_____ Date:_____

Exploring the Evidence: Grading Sheet

TOPIC _____

Criterion	Mastering (9–10 points)	Accomplishing (6–8 points)	Learning (0–5 points)
Demonstrates knowledge of topic ____ x 4 = ____	• included 30 or more relevant facts • in-depth and detailed in explanation • main ideas clearly stated so that audience has a clear understanding of the material	• included between 20 and 30 facts, most of which were relevant • somewhat in-depth and detailed in explanation • main ideas stated so that audience has a limited understanding of the material	• included less than 20 facts, some of which were relevant • lacked depth and detail in explanation • main ideas stated in a confusing, unfocused way so audience does not understand material
Organization of presentation ____ x 2 = ____	• included a thorough, thoughtfully planned introduction, body, and conclusion • moved smoothly from one topic to another • professional and prepared	• included a planned introduction, body, and conclusion • moved smoothly from one topic to another for the most part • could be more professional and prepared	• included a weak introduction, body, and/or conclusion, or none at all • transitions from one topic to another were jumpy and random • not professional or prepared
Experiment, activity, visual ____ x 2 = ____	• completed experiment(s), demonstration(s), or prepared a visual that clearly, thoroughly, and accurately communicates most significant information in the presentation • enhanced presentation • students gained a clearer understanding of the topic as a result • creative • reflected high-level thinking and effort	• completed experiment(s), demonstration(s), or prepared a visual that communicates some of the information in the presentation • somewhat enhanced presentation • students gained a clearer understanding of part of the topic as a result • somewhat creative • could have made additions to project to increase level of thinking	• completed experiment(s), demonstration(s), or prepared a visual that does not communicate most significant information in the presentation • did not enhance presentation • students did not gain a clearer understanding of the topic as a result • low-level thinking, simple
References	• used a minimum of four sources, at least two books and two Web sites (or one expert) • correctly documented with no errors	• used three sources • documented with minimal errors	• used less than three sources • documented with many errors
Note sheet	• appropriate for topic/presentation • followed order of presentation • user friendly—easy to complete • thoroughly reflected main topics	• somewhat appropriate for topic/presentation • somewhat followed order of presentation • a little confusing to complete • reflected many of the main topics	• not appropriate for topic/presentation • did not follow order of presentation • difficult to complete • did not reflect main topics

Total_____/100

© Prufrock Press Inc. • *Crime Scene Detective: Arson*
This page may be photocopied or reproduced with permission for student use.

Crime Scene Simulation

Overview

A crime scene simulation gives the students the opportunity to practice the skills they have been studying. If you do not want to use this simulation, you may design a crime scene that is unique for your school. Instructions for writing your own simulation begin on p. 87. The crime scene can be as detailed and in-depth as you choose it to be. It can have as little as 3 pieces of evidence or more than 10 pieces of evidence. You may have 10 people involved or the entire teaching staff. The location will depend on your crime. Each suspect must have reason to have visited the crime scene area. It is best to have it in an area that students can easily access, such as a library.

This section includes witness statements and storylines for a crime that involves arson in the school library. Supporting materials such as forensic lab procedures, a suspect identification card, and a sample news article are also provided. Many of these materials can serve as examples for writing materials for your own simulation.

Roles

The crime scene simulation provided was written for and used in a middle school with approximately 75 faculty and staff members. More than 45 people volunteered to participate. If you don't want to start off that big or if you do not have enough staff members to fill the roles, you could limit the number of people who are suspects. You must, however, use the profile for Suspect 1, as this person was designated the guilty party. You must also use Suspect 6, the person who spotted and reported the fire.

It is important that you talk with and get the approval of this simulation with your principal. He or she can play a big role in the simulation (one of the suspects is the principal). Usually, if the principal is involved and supportive of your simulation, other teachers and staff members also will be supportive and involved.

Roles for this simulation include suspects, witnesses who suspect others, character witnesses, and forensic lab technicians. Assign roles based on the number of participants. In this simulation, roles for six suspects were created. Each suspect had several people who suspected him or her (witnesses) and several people who thought he or she could never commit such a crime and/ or could provide an alibi for the suspect (character witnesses). Some of the suspect stories were based on the unique characteristics of the people and situations in my particular school. Other stories were simply made up. You can use these sample stories as they are written, alter them, or create new ones to fit your specific situation. Faculty and staff members were specifically chosen from all grade levels along with the secretarial and administrative staff. This required students to interview almost everyone in the school.

Motive

This simulation involves a fire that was started on purpose. Arson makes a great crime to simulate because there are seven possible motives to work with. The motives are:

1. vanity—wanting to be the hero, save people, or get public recognition;
2. crime concealment—hiding a theft or other crime;
3. juvenile—kids under the age of 16 setting a fire for kicks;
4. insurance fraud—for financial gain, often the case in a failing business;
5. pyromania—an uncontrollable desire to set a destructive fire;
6. civil disorder—burning down a church, government office, or abortion clinic; and
7. spite or revenge—burning down someone's house or business to get revenge.

Introduce the motives to your students prior to beginning the simulation. See Appendix B (see p. 92) for a fact sheet that may be made into a transparency.

Recruiting Participants

Ask for volunteers from your faculty and staff to play the various roles. Your crime scene storylines will depend on how many volunteers you get to participate. Based on this number, determine how many suspects you will have. Each suspect will have at least three people with collaborating stories pointing to the guilt of the suspect and two people to serve as character witnesses, claiming the suspect must certainly be innocent of the crime or providing the suspect with an alibi. Delete suspects or forensic lab technicians to accommodate the number of staff members who are willing to participate. Fill out the chart on p. 43 with the participants' names. Be sure that students do not see this chart. *Note:* The school nurse and office staff make great forensic lab technicians. Students can visit them during class time without interrupting another teacher's instructional time.

Storylines

Each storyline is developed to make the suspect appear to be the guilty party. It is only by viewing the evidence that students will be able to determine the guilt of a suspect. Because students only receive facts in bits and pieces at a time, it isn't obvious that a person is a suspect until several people have been interviewed. In the same way, a detective won't know if a suspect has an alibi until he or she interviews the character witnesses. The storylines unfold as more people are interviewed.

Storylines are open ended to encourage students to speculate and draw conclusions. Some of the actions of some of the suspects are never explained. The suspects themselves may make up something to justify any behavior or action that isn't previously explained in their storyline. For example, why did Suspect 2 take paint thinner out of the art room? The only thing that sets the guilty person apart is the physical evidence left behind.

Although some of the storylines may seem unlikely or unusual, students and staff members alike love them. Remember, you are dealing with kids and teachers—the stranger the better.

Keeping the Secret

When you initially assign roles, don't tell anyone who the guilty person is. Only you and the guilty person should know the truth. It may sway witnesses' statements if they know who committed the crime, and it is bound to get back to the students.

Preparing Materials

Duplicate the following materials and give them to the appropriate people:
- Give each witness a copy of the:
  o newspaper article (see p. 44),
  o witness role description (see p. 45), and
  o witness information sheet (this contains the storylines for all witnesses who suspect a given suspect and is different for each witness).
- Give each suspect and the guilty person a copy of the:
  o newspaper article (see p. 44);
  o suspect role description (see p. 46);
  o suspect profile (different for each person; begins on p. 50);
  o witness information sheet for each specific suspect (this contains the storylines for all witnesses who suspect a given suspect); and
  o request for evidence samples (see pp. 47–48).

Getting Evidence From Suspects

Prior to setting up the crime scene, gather evidence from all identified suspects. Ask each suspect to complete a Suspect Identification Card (see p. 49). Take a picture with a digital camera and include it on the card. You may choose to assign a blood type to each suspect. This identification will be kept on file in the fingerprint lab. Ask for a hair sample and tape it to a note card.

Ask for each person to bring in a right-foot shoe. Photograph the bottom of the shoe, placing a ruler in the picture to determine an accurate scale. Print the picture and label it with the name of the person to whom it belongs. You will be leaving prints behind at the scene for the guilty person, so make sure you "stamp" the shoe of the guilty person before returning it (see Setting Up the Crime Scene, p. 38). Get a handwriting sample from each suspect for a note that is found at the scene, using the sample sheet on p. 48. Have the guilty person write the same list on a plain sheet of paper, as well. On the plain sheet of paper, he or she should only write the items on the list, not his or her name.

You will need to get two samples of fingerprints, hair, and handwriting from the guilty party. One set will be left at the crime scene, and the second set will be placed in the lab.

Setting Up the Forensic Labs

The number of labs you establish will depend on the number of volunteers you have. You may keep all of the evidence in one location or in a couple of rooms. It is best to have at least two different locations so more students can view evidence at the same time with less congestion. For example, the students may view fingerprints and footprints in the same lab but go to another location to view handwriting and hair samples. Post a sign outside the door identifying the location as a forensic lab.

This simulation uses six labs—a fire report, blood, handwriting, hair, shoe print, and fingerprints. Although the evidence may all be viewed in the same lab, you will need to set up a separate file for each type of evidence.

On the outside of a file folder write the type of evidence (fingerprints, shoe prints, etc.). In the folder place the official report for that specific piece of evidence and any physical evidence recovered from the crime scene. Keep each suspect's evidence samples in separate envelopes and use one envelope for each type of evidence. Label each file folder with the type of evidence it contains. For example, the file folder labeled "Fingerprints" will contain all of the suspects' fingerprint samples in separate envelopes. This file folder and its contents will always remain in the possession of the lab technician. By organizing evidence this way, the lab technician can hand the students the information recovered from the crime scene without showing them all of the suspects' evidence samples. At the time they visit the lab, detectives may not know who all of the suspects are, so you don't want them to see all of the suspects' evidence. The lab technician will just give the students the evidence sample from the suspect they've requested.

After arriving at the lab, students will need to fill in the Forensic Lab Evidence Log (see p. 80). Make several copies of the log sheet and staple them to the inside of a folder. You should have one folder per lab. This log documents that the students have handled the evidence in question. If you have more than one class doing the simulation at the same time, you may have a different folder for each class to ensure confidentiality during the investigation. Give the lab technician a copy of the procedures for viewing evidence (see pp. 81–82). *Note*: A magnifying glass or microscope located at the lab is helpful for students viewing the trace evidence.

Setting up the Crime Scene

Choose an area in the school that would be appropriate for your storyline. This should be an area that is easily accessible to all suspects. In this simulation, the arson took place in the school library. Ask your local police department for crime scene tape to section off the crime scene or use another type of brightly colored tape. Decide what types of evidence would fit with your crime. Consult the Arson Lab Report on p. 84 to make sure the scene and evidence are set according to your police report. Here are a few suggestions for creating and placing evidence at the arson crime scene (you do not have to use all this evidence):

- *Footprints*—Paint the bottom of the guilty party's shoe, "stamp" it on black construction paper, and place it around the crime scene.
- *Fingerprints*—Have the guilty party put his or her prints on a piece of note card, trim around the prints, and place them at the scene.
- *Hair*—Put a few strands of hair on the sticky side of a piece of clear tape and place it at the scene. You might want to place it at the height of the guilty person.
- *Note*—Use the list that has the same words found on p. 48 written in the guilty party's handwriting. Place it where it is sure to be found. Burn around the edges of the paper to make it look like it was in the fire.
- *Fiber*—Place a small piece of fabric or other fiber-based material in a strategic location. You can create your own suspect samples from scraps of fabrics.
- *Books*—Choose books or other materials that could have been used to start the fire. Choose a few old books and burn them around the edges. Barbecuing them over a grill works nicely.

- *Glass*—Find a glass surface at the crime scene (window, overhead, copy machine, coffee pot, microwave oven) on which you can draw small cracks. Lots of small cracks (crazing) indicate a hot, fast fire, which means an accelerant was used. Because the arson report for this simulation calls for a copy machine to be near the burnt books, try to pick a location for your crime scene near a copy machine. Make sure you draw crazing cracks with nonpermanent marker on the glass on the copy machine.
- *Blood*—A small amount of a red substance left on a tissue or the floor could indicate blood.
- *Fire damage*—Use black bulletin board paper to cover areas indicating where the fire took place. Save the ashes from your fireplace or grill and spread them around, taking care not to put them where they could soil carpeting or other surfaces.

Remember that all of this evidence is circumstantial. Students still will have to analyze the statements of witnesses, establish a motive, and build a strong case to prove the person guilty.

Planting Evidence

When you determine what evidence you will be using, you will need to plant some of it in the guilty person's room. For example, you might hide a bottle of acetone on a bookshelf where student detectives could find it when conducting a search of the suspect's room. Or, if you burned books to use in the crime scene, you might leave some of the books in the suspect's room.

Viewing the Crime Scene

Let teachers and staff know that the investigation has begun. They can review their statements and be prepared for an interview. Before taking students to the crime scene, distribute the newspaper article concerning the alleged crime. You can fill in the empty spaces on p. 44 or you can write an article that is more specific to your school. If you fill in the provided article, be sure to write the name of the librarian in the third blank and the name of Suspect 6 in the fourth blank. Read and discuss the article. Ask students to predict what types of evidence they may see or what they may be looking for. Review the police procedures at a crime scene previously discussed in class.

Take students to the crime scene. Have them first sketch the room. After completing this, they may look around the room without touching anything. You don't want any evidence destroyed. When sketching the room, students should record the pieces of possible evidence they have found. Give everyone a significant amount of time to view the scene.

Discuss the evidence found at the scene, reviewing the difference between circumstantial and direct evidence. Ask for student volunteers to mark each piece of evidence with some sort of indicator such as an orange cone. You can easily make cones out of construction paper. At this time, you could also have students take measurements from each piece of evidence to two different fixed objects in the room. Take pictures of the crime scene with a digital camera. If you have access to a computer, place these pictures into a file on the computer or print them out so that students can always have access to the crime scene even after you take it down.

Use any remaining class time to generate ideas of who may have committed the crime, to discuss possible motives (remember the seven motives for starting a fire), and to develop a plan of action for proceeding with the investigation.

Student Procedures for Solving the Crime

If you have more than one class working on the case, make each class a different police precinct. A competition between the classes to see who can solve the case first adds to the excitement. Be sure to keep the investigation of each class confidential.

Students should not be told which faculty members are participating. Just like in real life, a list of suspects isn't left behind at the crime scene. After visiting the crime scene, students may want to read through the news article again. This article will give the students a few ideas of where to begin. Usually students will begin interviewing people they know well. Sometimes they will get a lead that pays off, sometimes they won't.

As a class decide which students will interview which staff members. Students should work in pairs to make sure all information from the interview gets noted. Students should always be prepared for an interview by taking with them a list of predetermined questions and paper and pen to record answers.

Questioning Procedures

Conducting interviews with faculty and staff members is a difficult skill. Be sure to spend time discussing the types of questions that will get desired answers. Students should avoid asking "yes" or "no" questions. A student should not ask, "Did you start the fire?" because a guilty person would naturally answer the question with a "no." Instead, students should ask questions like, "Where were you on the day or time of the fire?", "Do you know anyone who might have a motive for doing this?", and "Have you noticed anyone behaving suspiciously or out of character?" A favorite follow-up question is, "What's the worst thing that will happen to you if you tell the truth?" Sometimes you can catch a person off guard with that question. As a class, brainstorm a list of questions that would be appropriate to ask. Narrow this list down to a maximum of 10 questions, ordering them in an appropriate manner. Have the students write down these questions for future reference. Additional questions not on the original list may need to be asked while the investigation is underway.

It will be beneficial to the students to practice interviewing each other before interviewing teachers and staff members. Encourage the students to ask follow-up questions as new information becomes available during the interview. Make sure each student has paper for recording statements. Remind the students that they should be polite and considerate of those they are interviewing at all times.

Students should set up times to interview staff members before or after school, during lunch, or during planning time. Before interviewing anyone, students should identify themselves as a detective from your classroom.

Teacher's Role

Your role in the investigation is that of sergeant. You will not participate in interviewing witnesses, interpreting evidence, or anything else that might influence the students' opinions or tactics. It is your job to help keep them on track and help them organize the information.

One of your duties is to create a master list of all staff members, leaving enough room for students to record the staff members' statements. As a class, decide which pair of student detectives is going to interview which staff member. When students report back to the class after an interview, record the information they received from that person on the master list. You will need a separate list and file for each class participating in the simulation.

Once students begin identifying possible suspects, it may help to write the suspect's name on a large sheet of paper. Write things such as possible motive, witness statements, and alibis on this paper as the information comes in. Display the information in the room. This is a great visual for students to help them process all of the incoming information. If you do this simulation with more than one class, be sure to take down the posters before the next class comes in.

After a student interviews a staff member, it is possible he or she will not get all of the testimony available. This may be due to the student not asking the right questions to get the desired answers or it could be that the staff member forgot his or her part. You may need to redirect the student back to the staff member for another interview suggesting different questions or you may need to kindly remind the staff member to re-read the witness statement.

Examining Evidence at the Lab

When, in your opinion, students have interviewed enough people and have a sufficient amount of evidence pointing to a suspect, you may let them complete an Evidence Request Card (see p. 79) that allows them to go to the designated forensic labs to see the physical evidence.

Students must have established probable cause to view evidence at the forensic lab. In real life, police don't have records on every person in the world. The same is true here. Students can't just ask to see fingerprints and hair samples from every teacher in the school.

On the request cards, student detectives must list the type of evidence they are requesting, the suspect they are requesting it for, and justify why that person is a suspect. Only with teacher approval can they proceed to the lab. Once approved, they go to the lab, give the card to the lab technician, and then view the evidence. They may only see the evidence found at the crime scene and the evidence of the suspect that has been approved. After visiting the lab, students report their findings back to the class. When visiting a lab, it is best to send the students in smaller groups or with a partner. The number you send at one time will depend on the size and location of your lab. It generally does not work well to send the entire class at the same time.

Charging a Suspect—Conclusion

Students may charge a suspect with the crime when they have interviewed the majority of the key witnesses, gathered enough information, and have sufficient physical evidence. If you are not going to have a mock trial, then you may tell the students if they are right at this point in the simulation. You could also have students present the case to you as if they were prosecuting attorneys. This could be a written statement or oral presentation.

If you are going to hold a mock trial, do not tell the class if they charged the right person. It will be up to the mock trial jury to decide the guilt or innocence of the charged. After the jury has made its decision, you may reveal the name of the guilty person.

Additional Assessment

Have students write a detective report describing what they witnessed, who they talked to, who they suspect and why, and their interpretation of the evidence. This could be a daily or weekly report (see p. 78).

Timeline of Events

This simulation assumes the crime takes place on a Wednesday and that the school dismissal time is 3 p.m. You may need to adjust the times based on the dismissal time of your school.

Chart of Roles in the Simulation

In the chart below, fill in the names of the people who will play these roles. This simulation has six suspects. To involve fewer people, you can eliminate some of the suspects and the accompanying witnesses. *Note*: Suspect 1 is the guilty party and Suspect 6 is the person who first saw and reported the fire. You should not eliminate these two suspects. Also be sure to read the suspect profiles carefully when assigning the roles. Each profile's language contains specific gender usage. This can easily be changed on your end, depending on who volunteers, or you may wish to assign roles based on the genders portrayed in the suspect profiles.

Suspects	People Who Suspect This Person	Character Witnesses
Suspect 1	a. b. c. d.	a. b.
Suspect 2	a. b. c.	a. b.
Suspect 3	a. b. c.	a. b.
Suspect 4	a. b. c. d.	a. b.
Suspect 5	a. b. c.	a. b.
Suspect 6	a. b. c.	a. b.
Lab Technician		
Lab Technician		
Lab Technician		

THE DAILY PRESS

Volume 1 Issue V

School Library Burns
Police Still Investigating Cause of Wednesday Fire

At approximately 3:50 p.m. on Wednesday, the _____ Fire Department was called to _____ School. When firefighters arrived at the scene, they found the library in flames. Firefighters worked quickly to put out the fire. Officials are investigating the possibility of arson.

Fortunately, no one was injured, as the students and many of the teachers had already left school for the day. The librarian, _____, said, "This is just tragic. We won't know the full extent of our loss for several days. Tomorrow I was going to begin my inventory. I don't understand what could have happened."

Teacher, _____, was at the scene. She saw the fire and called 911. She said, "I was just walking by the library when I saw this thick, black smoke. I ran back to my classroom and called 911. I can't imagine what would have happened if I had not been there. I knew I was risking my own life by staying in the building to make the phone call, but I just had to report the fire, even if it meant putting my own life in danger."

Arson investigators were on the scene immediately. Chief Investigator Matthew Taylor said that the detectives will continue their investigation over the course of the next few days, inspecting the scene and gathering evidence. As it is collected, evidence will be transferred to the local forensic lab for analysis. He said that the detectives are currently investigating the case and will follow every lead until the cause of the fire is established and the guilty person is held accountable. "I have a good team of detectives," he said. "We will get to the bottom of this. If it is arson, we will find the guilty person."

© Prufrock Press Inc. • *Crime Scene Detective: Arson*
This page may be photocopied or reproduced with permission for student use.

Role Description: Witness

Thank you for volunteering to participate in this simulation. You have been assigned the role of a witness. Your statement will give either a firsthand account of the fire, background information on events that you believe led to the fire, or defend or accuse one of the suspects. All witnesses are friendly and are willing to help solve the crime. See the attached witness statement for your specific role.

As in a real investigation, students will initially have no clue as to who might be a witness or a suspect. They do not know which staff members are participating in the simulation. Please do not reveal that information to them. They will need to decide whom they should interview.

The newspaper article (see attached) is all the information students have when the simulation begins. Students must use their critical thinking skills to find and interview each person who volunteered to play a role.

Interviews

The detectives in the case will be interviewing various witnesses. Consult your witness information statement and answer the questions the detectives ask. The detectives must learn the fine art of questioning and ask questions that will uncover the answers they are looking for. It may be necessary for a detective to interview you more than once depending on the evidence that is revealed during the investigation.

Collaborating Witnesses

Each witness will have other witnesses or leads for the police. At the detectives' request, please give those names to the detectives. For instance, the detective may ask, "Can you think of anyone else who might have additional information or who can collaborate your theory?" You may supply your names at that time. These names may also come up in the course of your conversation.

Witness Statement

Please read your attached statement carefully and let me know if you have any questions. Make sure you give the information provided in your statement. The statements have been written to collaborate with other people's statements. In particular, if you have a direct quote from the suspect in your statement be sure to share the quote with the detectives.

All witness statements for a given suspect are included on the attached page. This will allow you to know what storyline your collaborating witnesses have been given. You may also elaborate on your statement as long as the content doesn't change.

There really is no right or wrong way to play this role. The main goal is that students get an idea of the steps detectives must go through to solve a case and that they get a chance to use their deductive reasoning and critical thinking skills.

Have fun and thanks so much for your help!

Role Description: Suspect

Thank you for volunteering to participate in this simulation. You will be a prime suspect in an arson case involving a fire in the school. Please do not tell other staff members you are a suspect. If they know this, it could sway their testimonies.

As in a real investigation, students will initially have no clue as to who might be a witness or a suspect. They do not know which staff members are participating in the simulation. Please do not reveal that information to them. They will need to decide whom they should interview.

The newspaper article (see attached) is all the information students have when the simulation begins. Students must use their critical thinking skills to find and interview each person who volunteered to play a role.

Interviews

The detectives in the case will be interviewing various witnesses. Some of these witnesses will believe that you might have a motive to commit such a crime. Not every witness will suspect you, so please do not share your profile with other participants. When a detective first interviews you, he or she may not realize that other people suspect you. Unless he or she asks you directly about being identified as a suspect, do not reveal your role.

Once the detectives realize you are a potential suspect, you must do your best to convince them you are innocent. This is where your acting skills come in. You may certainly send mixed messages by acting guilty while proclaiming your innocence to challenge the abilities of the detectives. You may try to discredit those witnesses who suspect you. You will also have a few people you can use as alibis or character witnesses. Feel free to give those names to the detectives to further support your claim of innocence.

Suspect Profile

Please read your attached profile carefully and let me know if you have any questions. The profile is general. Feel free to really get into your character by adding whatever character traits you think would make the simulation more believable.

There really is no right or wrong way to play this. The main goal is that students get an idea of the steps detectives must go through to solve a case and that they get a chance to use their deductive reasoning and critical thinking skills.

Witness Statements

Several staff members have good reason to believe you might be responsible for the fire. Attached are their storylines. It would be helpful for you to be familiar with their statements, as student detectives will be asking you about these storylines.

Have fun and thanks so much for your help!

© Prufrock Press Inc. • *Crime Scene Detective: Arson*
This page may be photocopied or reproduced with permission for student use.

Evidence Request: Suspect

As a prime suspect, several pieces of evidence are needed from you. As soon as you are identified as a suspect and the students have established probable cause, they will have access to your records at the local forensic lab. The following information details what is needed. Please complete the following tasks and return them in the envelopes provided.

Fingerprints—Fill out the Suspect Identification Card. I will be coming around with the digital camera to take your picture and attach it to the card. Use a black inkpad to stamp your fingerprints. If you need assistance, please let me know.

Hair Sample—Enclosed you will find an index card and a small envelope. Please cut two or three hairs from your head. Tape them to the index card. Return this with the other contents of this packet.

Handwriting Sample—On the Suspect Handwriting Sample sheet (see attached) give a handwriting sample by writing in *cursive* the words that are listed.

Shoe Print—Bring in a right-footed shoe that has unique markings on the sole. Put the shoe in a bag in my mailbox or drop it by my classroom. The bottom and side of the shoe will be photographed and then your shoe will be returned to you. The bottom of one person's shoe will also be painted and stamped to create a shoeprint for the crime scene, so please be sure to bring old shoes. Make sure to include your name on the shoe or in the bag so I can return each shoe to its owner.

Please return these items to me by _____.

Suspect Handwriting Sample

Please print your name on the line below:

_____

Please write your name in cursive on the line below:

_____

In the box provided, please write the following list, in cursive:

Lighter fluid
Matches
Kerosene
Fire extinguisher
Milk
Bread

┌─────────────────────────────┐
│   │
│   │
│   │
│   │
│   │
│   │
│   │
│   │
│   │
│   │
└─────────────────────────────┘

This is an official document and is the property of the Forensic Lab.

Suspect Handwriting Sample

Please print your name on the line below:

_____

Please write your name in cursive on the line below:

_____

In the box provided, please write the following list, in cursive:

Lighter fluid
Matches
Kerosene
Fire extinguisher
Milk
Bread

┌─────────────────────────────┐
│   │
│   │
│   │
│   │
│   │
│   │
│   │
│   │
│   │
│   │
└─────────────────────────────┘

This is an official document and is the property of the Forensic Lab.

© Prufrock Press Inc. • *Crime Scene Detective: Arson*
This page may be photocopied or reproduced with permission for student use.

Suspect Identification Card

Attach suspect's photo here.

last name: _____

first name: _____

date of birth:_____

sex: _____

height: _____ blood type: _____

eye color:_____ hair color:_____

Fingerprint Record

Right Hand

Thumb	Index	Middle	Ring	Little

Left Hand

Thumb	Index	Middle	Ring	Little

This is an official document and is the property of the Forensic Lab.

© Prufrock Press Inc. • *Crime Scene Detective: Arson*
This page may be photocopied or reproduced with permission for student use.

Suspect 1 Profile

Suspect 1:

You are *guilty* of starting the fire in the library. Don't divulge this information to anyone.

Your Story

You enjoy teaching. Working with the students is OK, but you have always thought the fun part about teaching science is experimenting with chemicals and fire. Because of your enthusiasm (really, it's an obsession) for fire, some people might consider you a pyromaniac.

On two separate occasions this year, the fire alarm was actually activated. When the fire department arrived the first time, they determined that the cause was excessive smoke from an "experiment" that you were conducting in your room. You don't think this is out of the ordinary—after all, conducting experiments can only enhance your students' educational experience.

On the second occasion, a small fire took place in the teacher's lounge. You "accidentally" burned food wrapped in foil in the microwave. You claim you were trying to determine the point at which foil burns and just let the experiment get out of hand. When the faculty was debriefed at a later meeting, you weren't really remorseful at all. As a matter of fact, you were quite excited. You continued to talk about the sparks that flew out of the microwave, the flames, and the fire trucks. You couldn't have been happier. Some people may think you are strange, but you are a science teacher, after all!

On Wednesday, the day of the fire, three teachers (see attached witness storylines) were chatting in the commons area before school when you walked by carrying several large boxes of matches and a bottle of acetone. They think you may have used the materials to start the fire in the library.

Several staff members believe you could have started the fire in the library because of your fascination with fire. *Carefully read the attached witness testimonies for your additional storylines.*

In case the detectives should ask, you have the following chemicals in your classroom: phosphorous, benzine, sulfuric acid, iodine, and acetone.

Tell students you don't remember what time you left school on the day of the fire. You think it was around 3:15 p.m. No one saw you leave, and you can't remember what you did that day after school.

Here's the tricky part: Until the detectives learn that someone suspects you, don't tip them off. They may come to you initially to get information about the fire. Just say you don't know anything about it. Don't defend yourself until you are actually accused. The detectives will be back as soon as they have a lead. _____ and _____ will be good character witnesses for you. They believe you would never be capable of doing this. Mention their names to the detectives if you need someone to help defend you.

© Prufrock Press Inc. • *Crime Scene Detective: Arson*
This page may be photocopied or reproduced with permission for student use.

Witnesses Who Suspect _____ (Suspect 1)

Witness 1A: _____

Witness 1B: _____

Witness 1C: _____

Witness 1D: _____

You are among several staff members (those listed above) who believe
_____ (Suspect 1) may have been involved in the fire. You
are suspicious because you think he is a pyromaniac.

You have worked with _____ (Suspect 1) for several
years. You believe that teaching science is right up his alley because of his
fascination with chemicals and fires. It seems as if he is obsessed with burning
things, under the guise of conducting educational experiments, of course.

On two separate occasions this year, the fire alarm was actually activated.
When the fire department arrived the first time, they determined that the
cause was excessive smoke from an "experiment" that _____
(Suspect 1) was conducting in his room.

On the second occasion, a small fire took place in the teacher's lounge.
_____ (Suspect 1) admitted to "accidentally" burning food
wrapped in foil in the microwave. He claims he was trying to determine the
point at which foil burns and just let the experiment get out of hand. When
the faculty was debriefed at a later meeting, _____ (Suspect
1) didn't seem remorseful at all! As a matter of fact, he was quite excited. He
continued to talk about the sparks that flew out of the microwave, the flames, and
the fire trucks. He couldn't have been happier. You thought that was extremely odd.

On Wednesday, the day of the fire, _____,
_____, and _____ (Witnesses 1A, 1B, and
1C) were chatting in the commons area before school when
_____ (Suspect 1) walked by carrying several large boxes of
matches and a bottle of acetone. You all jokingly commented that he was a
pyromaniac. Later when you heard about the library fire, _____'s
(Suspect 1) name immediately popped into your head.

When the detectives interview you, share your concerns with them. *Be sure
to mention your unique observations as listed on the next page.* You may also share
the names of the others on the above list to support your theory. Feel free to
read directly off your paper if you need to, to ensure that the information is
given accurately.

If you don't know how to answer a question, you can always say, "I
just don't know," or "I don't remember," or make up something *reasonable*.
Sometimes people who know the same person will give conflicting reports
about that person. Sorting through all of the testimony is just part of the
detectives' job. Just remember that you suspect _____
(Suspect 1) was involved and your answers and statements should reflect that
suspicion.

Special Notes for Witnesses Who Suspect

_____ (Suspect 1)

Witness 1A:

Throughout the school year, you've walked into _____'s (Suspect 1) room before and after school to discover that he was conducting science experiments involving fire. Although it seemed a little dangerous, you thought it was great that he would enhance his teaching by preparing these experiments. When you mentioned this to him he said, _"The experiments aren't for my students. I just really enjoy playing with fire."_ Be sure to share that quote with the detectives.

You thought he was joking but when you pressed him about this comment, he suddenly didn't want to discuss it further. You remember on more than one occasion smelling smoke coming from his classroom. It was just earlier this year that the fire alarm was activated because an "experiment" he conducted produced too much smoke.

Witness 1B:

You were walking down the hallway around 3:15 p.m. on the day of the fire when you smelled smoke. You went to investigate. You thought it was coming from _____'s (Suspect 1) room, and when you got there he seemed very upset that you came into his room. You couldn't help but notice he was working with several bottles of chemicals—you aren't sure what kind. He also had matches and a stack of paperback books. You didn't see the titles of the books and you can't be sure, but it almost looked like he had poured some of the chemicals on the books.

He quickly put everything into a box, dismissed the smoky smell, ushered you out of his room, and took off walking. You heard him mutter under his breath, _"Where can a guy go for privacy around here?"_ Be sure to share that comment with the detectives.

About 5 minutes later you saw _____ (Suspect 1) walk into the library. He was carrying that same box. He wasn't in the mood to stop and talk to you. You noticed he seemed particularly nervous.

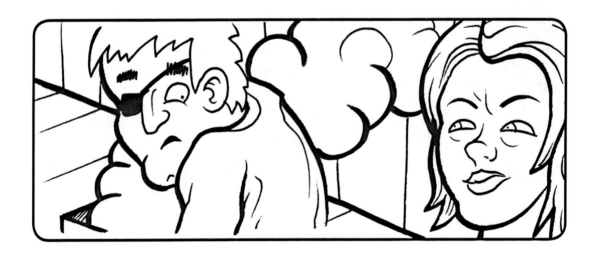

© Prufrock Press Inc. • _Crime Scene Detective: Arson_
This page may be photocopied or reproduced with permission for student use.

Witness 1C:

During the course of the year, you've had concerns about
_____'s (Suspect 1) behavior. The last science curriculum meeting was held in his room. You couldn't help but notice the countertop was charred in several places. When you asked him about it, he said it was just an experiment "gone bad." You also noticed a lot of candles, matches, and chemicals. In fact, during the meeting he continued to strike matches against the table and then burn small bits of paper in a trashcan. He would just stare at the flame and smile. You thought it was weird, but you didn't say anything. Given the history of the fires at school and his bizarre behavior, you think he may be responsible for the fire in the library.

Witness 1D:

On the day of the fire, you were walking by the library. You saw
_____ (Suspect 1) walking out of the library *empty-handed*. Be sure to emphasize that he was not carrying anything. You think it was about 3:35 p.m. He seemed to be very distracted and in a bit of a hurry. You said hello to him, but he just took off running.

Character Witnesses for _____ (Suspect 1)

Character Witness 1A: _____

Character Witness 1B: _____

Several staff members suspect _____ (Suspect 1) was involved in some way in the fire. You are a character witness for _____ (Suspect 1).

You know nothing about the fire or the crime scene. If a detective questions you about the crime scene itself, you know that the fire was in the library and that's it.

Here's the tricky part: When you are first interviewed by a detective, he or she may not suspect _____ (Suspect 1), so don't defend his character until the detectives ask you specifically about him.

When the detectives ask you about _____ (Suspect 1), please elaborate in your own words, making up things about him that would lead the students to believe he is a wonderful person who would do nothing wrong. Some ideas to bring up include the following: you have known him for years; you know he could never do anything like this; every time you see him he is so nice—he always has a kind word to say; he has told you how much he enjoys working with all of the teachers and students here; he is such a conscientious person; he is so dedicated; and so forth.

If you don't know how to answer a question, you can always say, "I just don't know," or "I don't remember." Sometimes people who know the same person will give conflicting reports about that person. Sorting through all of the testimony is just part of the detective's job. Just remember you are in _____'s (Suspect 1) corner.

© Prufrock Press Inc. • *Crime Scene Detective: Arson*
This page may be photocopied or reproduced with permission for student use.

Suspect 2 Profile

Suspect 2: _____

Your Story

Although you love teaching, playing and singing with your band are your first passions. You would love to quit teaching and take your "show on the road." Your band has been playing at local clubs but you just know you are ready for the big time. You believe you are a great singer and could even make it on your own.

When "American Idol" was auditioning in town you tried out, and although Paula thought you were cute, Simon and Randy didn't think you were "Idol" material and you weren't invited to go to Hollywood. You know they are wrong. If only the American public could see you or the band, you know they would feel differently. You know that getting local publicity is a great start to national exposure.

Tell the detectives you first learned about the fire on the night it occurred, while watching the evening news. You were trying to figure out how you could help out with this terrible tragedy. It occurred to you that you could raise money by performing a benefit concert and get exposure for your band at the same time. What a win-win situation.

You chose a date and a place for the concert and by the time you came back to school the next day, you had prepared several posters to place around the school announcing the upcoming concert. You even called the public relations department for the district in the hopes that they would do a feature story on you and the band.

On the day of the fire, you left school at 3:30 p.m. to go home. You don't think anyone saw you leave.

Several staff members suspect that you might have started the fire to get more attention for yourself and the band. They think it is suspicious that you've already developed a plan for a benefit concert and that you've already contacted the PR department. *Carefully read the attached witness testimonies for your additional storylines.*

Here's the tricky part: Until the detectives learn that someone suspects you, don't tip them off. They may come to you initially to get information about the fire. Just say you don't know anything about it. Don't defend yourself until you are actually accused. The detectives will be back as soon as they have a lead. _____ and _____ are character witnesses for you. They believe in you! Mention their names to the detectives if you need someone to help defend you.

© Prufrock Press Inc. • *Crime Scene Detective: Arson*
This page may be photocopied or reproduced with permission for student use.

Witnesses Who Suspect _____ (Suspect 2)

Witness 2A: _____

Witness 2B: _____

Witness 2C: _____

Although _____ (Suspect 2) loves teaching, playing and singing with his band are his first passions. You know _____ (Suspect 2) would love to quit teaching and take his "show on the road." His band has been playing at local clubs but _____ (Suspect 2) thinks he is ready for the big time. He believes he is a great singer and could even make it on his own.

When "American Idol" was auditioning in town, _____ (Suspect 2) tried out, and although Paula thought he was cute, Simon and Randy didn't think he was "Idol" material and he wasn't invited to go to Hollywood. _____ (Suspect 2) feels they are wrong and thinks that if the American public could see him or the band, they would feel differently. He believes that getting local publicity is a great start to national exposure.

On the day after the fire, _____ (Suspect 2) was putting up posters around the school advertising a benefit concert for the school. He and his band were going to perform at this concert. You even heard that he was talking to the public relations department for the district, hoping to get more exposure for this concert. He seemed to be more concerned about himself than the school, and you wonder if maybe he started the fire just to get attention for the band.

When the detectives interview you, share your concerns with them. *Be sure to mention your unique observations as listed on the next page.* You may also share the names of the others on the above list to support your theory. Feel free to read directly off your paper if you need to, to ensure that the information is given accurately.

If you don't know how to answer a question, you can always say, "I just don't know," or "I don't remember," or make up something *reasonable*. Sometimes people who know the same person will give conflicting reports about that person. Sorting through all of the testimony is just part of the detective's job. Just remember that you suspect _____ (Suspect 2) was involved and your answers and statements should reflect that suspicion.

© Prufrock Press Inc. • *Crime Scene Detective: Arson*
This page may be photocopied or reproduced with permission for student use.

Special Notes for Witnesses Who Suspect

_____ (Suspect 2)

Witness 2A:

You've worked with _____ (Suspect 2) for several years and you know how much he loves playing with his band. It is all he ever talks about during meetings or in the hallway. You've watched him play a few times, and you were impressed. He constantly tells you how he wants to hit the "big time." He is a huge fan of "American Idol" and always talks about the songs he would choose to sing on the show. He says he just needs one lucky break—he just needs the right person to see him perform. The more places his band plays, the greater the chances are of him being discovered.

On the morning of the fire, you saw _____ (Suspect 2) walking out of the art room with cans of paint thinner. When you asked him why he needed the paint thinner, he was very abrupt with you and told you it didn't concern you and to mind your own business. You thought he was acting very suspicious.

On the day after the fire, you arrived at school early. You noticed that _____ (Suspect 2) was already there. He was talking to a television news reporter about how his band would be performing a benefit concert to help replace things that were damaged in the fire. You thought this was very strange and you wonder if he might have started the fire for the opportunity to perform on TV with his band.

Witness 2B:

You know _____ (Suspect 2) was excited when he heard "American Idol" was coming to town. He immediately said he was going to audition. Simon is his hero. Because you are known for your work with school productions, _____ (Suspect 2) came to you for help with his stage presence. He just kept saying that he was going to be the next "American Idol." Later you found out that he didn't make it through to Hollywood. He was really bummed. Although Paula thought he did an OK job, Randy and Simon told him to keep his day job. He was determined to prove Simon and

Randy wrong. When you asked how he planned to do that, he said, *"It all starts with local publicity. TV is the way to go. I'll do whatever it takes to get the band on TV."* Please make sure you share these quotes with the students.

Now, he's planning a huge benefit concert. You wonder if he may have started the fire in order to get attention for the band and to prove Simon and Randy wrong.

Witness 2C:

You are also aware of _____'s (Suspect 2) obsession with his band. You often eat lunch with him in the staff lounge. You have heard all about his desire to be the next "American Idol" (see storylines above). You know that he has been working with _____ (Witness 2B) to develop his stage presence. He was so sure that he would be moving on to Hollywood and was extremely disappointed when he didn't make it. During lunch a few days before the fire, he was still talking about Simon's lack of ability to pick talent. He said, *"I just know that America wants me to be their next American Idol. The timing couldn't be better than this. I'm in my prime. I just need some publicity."* He went on to say, *"I will soon be proving Simon wrong. I have a plan to get the band on TV. I'll be singing in front of America before you know it."* When you asked him what his plan was, he would not elaborate. Please make sure you share these quotes with the students.

The day after the fire, you saw him at lunch hanging up his posters announcing his benefit concert. You couldn't help but think about your previous conversations and wonder if he had anything to do with the fire.

© Prufrock Press Inc. • *Crime Scene Detective: Arson*
This page may be photocopied or reproduced with permission for student use.

Character Witnesses for _____ (Suspect 2)

Character Witness 2A: _____

Character Witness 2B: _____

Several staff members suspect _____ (Suspect 2) was involved in some way in the fire. They believe he started the fire so he could give a benefit concert in order to get publicity for his band and for himself. (He tried out for "American Idol," but didn't make the final cut to Hollywood.) You are a character witness for _____ (Suspect 2).

You know nothing about the fire or the crime scene. If a detective questions you about the crime scene itself, you know that the fire was in the library and that's it.

Here's the tricky part: When the detectives first interview you, they may not suspect _____ (Suspect 2), so don't defend his character until the detectives ask you specifically about him.

When the police ask you about _____ (Suspect 2), please elaborate in your own words, making up things about him that would lead the police to believe he is a wonderful person who would do no wrong (e.g., you have taught with him for years, you know he could never do anything like this, he is so helpful and kind, and so on).

You do know that he is a dedicated musician who wants his band to go far. You also know that he wasn't chosen to go to Hollywood to be the next "American Idol." But, you don't think he would do anything illegal to promote his band or to get publicity for himself.

If you don't know how to answer a question, you can always say, "I just don't know," or "I don't remember." Sometimes people who know the same person will give conflicting reports about that person. Sorting through all of the testimony is just part of the detective's job. Just remember you are in _____'s (Suspect 2) corner.

Suspect 3 Profile

Suspect 3: _____

Your Story

As the school librarian, you are in charge of the school's books, videos, digital cameras, and other technology equipment. It is a huge responsibility being accountable for thousands of dollars worth of resources. You take your job very seriously.

You really get upset when teachers don't take the time to properly check out materials. You have streamlined the process so that it is really quite easy. What is wrong with the teachers who can't seem to follow the rules? After years of being the librarian, you believe some people are just thieves. Videos disappear. Books leave and never come back. You've even had a problem with digital cameras and video cameras. There are days when you just wish the teachers couldn't check out anything. It certainly would make your job much easier. You just don't have the time to be the "library police." You would much rather spend your time working with the students.

Several staff members believe you could have started the fire because you were tired of tracking down missing equipment. *Carefully read the attached witness testimonies for your additional storylines.*

On a separate note: You e-mailed the staff 4 days before the fire to let everyone know you would be taking inventory soon. On the day of the fire you left school at 3:10 p.m. to go to the grocery store. You did not lock the library when you left.

Here's the tricky part: Until the detectives learn that someone suspects you, don't tip them off. They may come to you initially to get information about the fire. Just say you don't know anything about it. Don't defend yourself until you are actually accused. The detectives will be back as soon as they have a lead. _____ and _____ will be character witnesses for you. They believe you would never be capable of doing this. Mention their names to the detectives if you need someone to help defend you.

© Prufrock Press Inc. • *Crime Scene Detective: Arson*
This page may be photocopied or reproduced with permission for student use.

Witnesses Who Suspect _____ (Suspect 3)

Witness 3A:
(librarian assistant or aide)

Witness 3B:

Witness 3C:

You are among several staff members (those listed above) who believe _____ (Suspect 3) may have been responsible for the fire. You believe she is mad at teachers for taking equipment and resources from the library without going through the proper check-out procedures and set the fire out of spite.

As the school librarian, _____ (Suspect 3) is in charge of the school's books, videos, digital cameras, and other technology equipment. It is a huge responsibility being accountable for thousands of dollars worth of resources. _____ (Suspect 3) takes her job very seriously.

She really gets upset when teachers don't take the time to properly check out materials. After years of being the librarian, you know she believes that some people are just thieves. Videos disappear. Books leave and never come back. She's even had a problem with digital cameras and video cameras. Some days, _____ (Suspect 3) says she just wishes the teachers couldn't check out anything. It certainly would make her job much easier. She complains that she just doesn't have the time to be the "library police." She would much rather spend her time working with the students.

When the detectives interview you, share your concerns with them. *Be sure to mention your unique observations as listed on the next page.* You may also share the names of the others on the above list to support your theory. Feel free to read directly off your paper if you need to, to ensure that the information is given accurately.

If you don't know how to answer a question, you can always say, "I just don't know," or "I don't remember," or make up something *reasonable*. Sometimes people who know the same person will give conflicting reports about that person. Sorting through all of the testimony is just part of the detective's job. Just remember that you suspect _____ (Suspect 3) was involved and your answers and statements should reflect that suspicion.

Special Notes for Witnesses Who Suspect

_____ (Suspect 3)

Witness 3A:

One of your responsibilities as a library assistant is to help teachers check out equipment. _____ (Suspect 3) has developed a very specific procedure for doing so and wants it to be strictly enforced. Lately you've noticed that when a few teachers came to check out certain movies, the videos were nowhere to be found. You checked the shelves and they weren't there, but no one has "officially" checked out the videos. When you investigated further you realized you have *more than 10 videos* unaccounted for. The same is true for the *digital cameras*. _____ (Witness 3B) wanted to check one out and when you went to get the camera, it wasn't in the cabinet. When you mentioned this to _____ (Suspect 3) she became very upset. She said, *"When I find out who is stealing this stuff I am going to make sure they never use the library again. Teachers just think they can walk in here and take whatever they want. I'm tired of it. They may think the check-out procedure is a hassle. I'll show them a hassle. What if they had nothing to check out at all?"* When you heard about the fire in the library media room, _____ (Suspect 3) immediately popped into your mind. Did she start the fire to get back at the teachers for abusing the system? Make sure you tell the detectives about her statement.

Witness 3B:

One day last week you wanted to check out a digital camera and went to the library to get one. _____ (Witness 3A) checked her computer system and saw that there were plenty in stock. When she went to the cabinet to get a camera, there weren't any cameras at all. She thought perhaps _____ (Suspect 3) had taken them so she mentioned the missing cameras to her while you were standing there. You were shocked at how mad _____ (Suspect 3) became. _____ (Suspect 3) said, *"When I find out who is stealing this stuff I am going to make sure they never use the library again. Teachers just think they can walk in here and take whatever they want. I'm tired of it. They may think the check-out procedure is a hassle. I'll show them a hassle. What if they had nothing to check out at all?"* You didn't know what to say, because _____ (Suspect 3) is usually so calm and nice. *Stealing*

© Prufrock Press Inc. • *Crime Scene Detective: Arson*
This page may be photocopied or reproduced with permission for student use.

seemed like such a strong word. You think this latest camera incident has put her over the edge. When you heard about the fire in the library media room, _____ (Suspect 3) immediately popped into your mind. Did she start the fire to get back at the teachers for abusing the system? Make sure you tell the detectives about her statement.

Witness 3C:

You often take your classes to the library for research. The last couple of times you've been in there you noticed _____ (Suspect 3) appeared to be upset and even angry. When you asked her if everything was OK, she confided in you. She said, *"I'm sick and tired of teachers taking materials and equipment without checking them out. We have digital cameras that are unaccounted for and several videos are missing, and there is no record of anyone checking them out. The process isn't that difficult. I don't think teachers realize how much work this is for me to track this stuff down. If I had my way, there wouldn't be any materials for teachers to check out. Then, maybe teachers would see the need to follow the procedures!"* Be sure to share her statements with the detectives. When you heard about the fire in the library media room you immediately thought that _____'s (Suspect 3) dream had come true—no more materials for teachers to check out.

Character Witnesses for_____ (Suspect 3)

Character Witness 3A: _____

Character Witness 3B: _____

Several staff members suspect _____ (Suspect 3) was involved in some way in the fire. You are a character witness for her. You know nothing about the fire or the crime scene. If a detective questions you about the crime scene itself, you know that the fire was in the library and that's it.

Here's the tricky part: When the detectives first interview you, they may not suspect _____ (Suspect 3). So, don't defend her character until the detectives ask you specifically about her.

When the detectives ask you about _____ (Suspect 3), please elaborate in your own words, making up things about her that would lead the police to believe she is a wonderful person who would do no wrong (e.g., you have worked with her for years; you know she could never do anything like this; she is so helpful, kind, gentle, and so on).

If you don't know how to answer a question, you can always say, "I just don't know" or "I don't remember." Sometimes people who know the same person will give conflicting reports about that person. Sorting through all of the testimony is just part of the detective's job. Just remember you are in _____'s (Suspect 3) corner.

Special Notes for Character Witnesses for _____ (Suspect 3)

Character Witness 3A: _____

On the morning after the fire, you saw _____ (Suspect 3) in the office. She was in tears just thinking about her poor library being destroyed. She was devastated. There is just no way someone who got that upset over the damage would have started the fire.

Character Witness 3B: _____

On the day of the fire, you bumped into _____ (Suspect 3) at the frozen food section at the nearby grocery store. You think the time was about 3:25 p.m. Be sure to mention this to the detectives. You might just be the alibi _____ (Suspect 3) needs.

© Prufrock Press Inc. • *Crime Scene Detective: Arson*
This page may be photocopied or reproduced with permission for student use.

Suspect 4 Profile

Suspect 4: _____

(principal)

Your Story

You enjoy your position as principal of the school. You have noticed, however, that over the years the district has become more financially strapped, making your job more difficult. It seems like every time you attend a principal's meeting you are told the same thing, *"Cut back on your expenses."*

You wish you could hire additional teachers to reduce class size. You wish you had more technology available in the building. Every teacher wants a smart board in his or her classroom and additional computers. Mounted projectors have become popular, and you wish you could put one in every classroom. The cost of ink for the school's printers is enough to put anyone in the poor house! There must be an easier way to get the much-needed funds for technology.

Being the innovative administrator you are, you start thinking outside of the box. You wonder about the district's insurance policy. If a tragedy such as a fire were to occur at your school, perhaps you could "pad" the school's current inventory—a few extra computers here, some advanced technology components there. It could mean additional funds for the school. No one would need to know.

Several staff members believe you could have started the fire in the library. *Carefully read the attached witness testimonies for your additional storylines.*

On the day of the fire, you had a meeting with a few staff members. The meeting started at 3:10 p.m. and ended at 3:30 p.m. You stayed around and chatted with _____ (Character Witness 4A) from 3:30 p.m. to about 3:45 p.m. _____ (Character Witness 4B) was in the office at the time and can confirm this meeting. Be sure to give these exact times, this just might be your alibi.

Here's the tricky part: Until our detectives learn that someone suspects you, don't tip them off. They may come to you initially to get information about the fire. Just say you don't know anything about it. Don't defend yourself until you are actually accused. The detectives will be back as soon as they have a lead.

_____ and _____ will be character witnesses for you. They believe in you! Mention their names to the detectives if you need someone to help defend you.

© Prufrock Press Inc. • *Crime Scene Detective: Arson*
This page may be photocopied or reproduced with permission for student use.

Witnesses Who Suspect _____ (Suspect 4)

Witness 4A: _____

Witness 4B: _____

Witness 4C: _____

Witness 4D: _____
(principal's secretary)

You are among several staff members (those listed above) who believe _____ (Suspect 4) may have been involved in the fire. Here is some background information.

_____ (Suspect 4) enjoys his position as principal. However, he has noticed over the years that the district has become more financially strapped, making his job more difficult. It seems like every time he attends a principal's meeting he is told the same thing, *"Cut back on your expenses."*

_____ (Suspect 4) wishes he could hire additional teachers to reduce class size. He wishes the school had more available technology in the building. Every teacher wants a smart board in his or her classroom and additional computers. Mounted projectors have become popular, and he wishes he could put one in every classroom. He's always saying that the cost of ink for the printers is enough to put anyone in the poor house! There must be an easier way to get the much-needed funds for technology.

You've all heard him voice the concerns above. You believe he may have started the fire to collect additional insurance money.

When the detectives interview you, share your concerns with them. *Be sure to mention your unique observations as listed on the next page.* You may also share the names of the others on the above list to support your theory. Feel free to read directly off your paper if you need to, to ensure that the information is given accurately.

If you don't know how to answer a question, you can always say, "I just don't know," or "I don't remember," or make up something *reasonable*. Sometimes people who know the same person will give conflicting reports about that person. Sorting through all of the testimony is just part of the detective's job. Just remember that you suspect _____ (Suspect 4) was involved in the fire and your answers and statements should reflect that suspicion.

© Prufrock Press Inc. • *Crime Scene Detective: Arson*
This page may be photocopied or reproduced with permission for student use.

Special Notes for Witnesses Who Suspect

_____ (Suspect 4)

Witness 4A:

Witness 4B:

You both serve on the technology committee. Your committee has been lamenting on the fact that you just don't have enough money to replace the older computers with new ones and to continue to buy new support equipment like smart boards, projectors, scanners, and printers. You have approached _____ (Suspect 4) on more than one occasion to voice your concern about the lack of money in the technology fund. In the past he has told you to prioritize the building needs and he'll just buy what he can. After the technology meeting held on the day before the fire, you both went together to once again approach _____ (Suspect 4) about getting additional funding. This time he said, _"Give me your complete wish list. I anticipate a certain event taking place that will provide additional funds for the school."_ Be sure to share this statement with the detectives.

When you asked him where the money was coming from, he said, _"Don't worry about where the money is coming from. I'll take care of it."_ Be sure to share this statement with the detectives. You thought that was really odd but you didn't pursue it further. Could this be related to the fire?

Witness 4C:

Being the team player that you are, people naturally gravitate to you to talk. _____ (Suspect 4) is no exception. Although you've worked with him for years, he seems different this year. The first semester, he complained a lot about budget cuts and was worried about buying technology items and other supplies for the school.

You met with the administrators one day last week. During your discussion, the budget for next year came up. You were shocked when _____ (Suspect 4) said that the technology budget was no longer a problem. When you asked about it, he simply said, _"Let's just say I've figured out a way to purchase additional equipment."_ When you asked him what he meant, he just said, _"Never mind."_ Make sure you share his statements with the detectives.

Witness 4D:

You've been _____'s (Suspect 4) secretary for several years now. You've been working with the building budget and have had many conversations with him about the diminishing funds. At first, the reduction in funds didn't seem to bother him, but you've noticed a change in him this year. He keeps complaining to you about the lack of money and is always asking, *"How much money do we have left now?"* As his secretary, you do a variety of work for _____ (Suspect 4) but his last request seemed odd to you. He wanted you to get a copy of the *school's insurance policy*. Being the good secretary that you are, you didn't question him, you just got a copy of the policy.

A few days later, he gave you a stack of handwritten receipts totaling thousands of dollars along with an additional inventory list. Some of the receipts were for computers, books, editing equipment, and other items. He said that this equipment was recently acquired and was in the building. He asked you to file the papers away. You were a little confused, because generally this kind of stuff goes through you and you don't remember completing purchase orders for it. You are wondering if the equipment that is on his list actually exists. When you questioned him about it he just said, *"Don't ask questions. Just do as I say and forget this conversation ever took place."* When you heard about the fire, you couldn't help but think about _____ (Suspect 4), the insurance policy, and his receipts. Be sure to share his statements with the detectives.

© Prufrock Press Inc. • *Crime Scene Detective: Arson*
This page may be photocopied or reproduced with permission for student use.

Character Witnesses for_____ (Suspect 4)

Character Witness 4A:

Character Witness 4B:

Several staff members suspect _____ (Suspect 4) was involved in some way in the fire. You are a character witness for him. You know nothing about the fire or the crime scene. If a detective questions you about the crime scene itself, you know that the fire was in the library and that's it.

Here's the tricky part: When the detectives first interview you, they may not suspect _____ (Suspect 4). So, don't defend his character until the detectives ask you specifically about him.

When the detectives ask you about _____ (Suspect 4), please elaborate in your own words, making up things about him that would lead the police to believe he is a wonderful person who would do no wrong (e.g., you have worked with him for years, you know he could never do anything like this, he has told you how much he enjoys working with all of the teachers and students here, he is such a conscientious person, he is so dedicated, and so on).

If you don't know how to answer a question, you can always say, "I just don't know" or "I don't remember." Sometimes people who know the same person will give conflicting reports about that person. Sorting through all of the testimony is just part of the detective's job. Just remember you are in _____'s (Suspect 4) corner.

Special Notes for Character Witnesses for_____ (Suspect 4)

Character Witness 4A:

On the day of the fire, _____ (Suspect 4) had a meeting with a few staff members. The meeting started at 3:10 p.m. and ended at 3:30 p.m. You stayed around and chatted with _____ (Suspect 4) from 3:30 p.m. to about 3:45 p.m. Be sure to give these exact times—you could be his alibi.

Character Witness 4B:

You were in the office and are aware of the meeting that took place after school and saw _____ (Character Witness 4A) and _____ (Suspect 4) chatting until about 3:45 p.m. Be sure to give these exact times—you could be his alibi.

Suspect 5 Profile

Suspect 5: _____

Your Story

You really enjoy teaching but have always been frustrated with the layout and design of your classroom. Who actually designed this school? You are sure that the architect paid more attention to the cost factor than the kid factor. Every classroom in this school is too small. In your dream world your classroom would have lots of storage space; a large teacher work area complete with a telephone; room for lots of computers and independent learning areas; space for kids to spread out and work; and yes, even a sink.

It is bad enough that you teach in a cracker box, but the library is even worse. It is difficult to take a class to use the library without students falling all over each other. There is no room to spread out when doing research and storage space for teacher resources is scarce. Books, technology, and other equipment are shoved into every nook and cranny, making it difficult to find and check out books.

You are a big fan of the TV show "Extreme Makeover: Home Edition" and think that it is just wonderful what Ty and his design team do to help others. Last week's episode was on a family who lost everything due to a terrible fire. Ty came in and saved the day designing and building a wonderful house for a very deserving family. This got you thinking: Why not "Extreme Makeover: School Edition?" Who wouldn't want to help out children and schools in their time of need?

You have voiced your concern and frustrations about the facilities to anyone who would listen. You recently shared with a few staff members your idea of nominating the school for an Extreme Makeover. You hope Ty and the producers will love the idea. You also believe that it would help your cause if some type of tragedy would occur at the school.

On the day of the fire, you left school around 3:30 p.m. You aren't sure if anyone saw you leave.

Several staff members suspect you may have started the fire to destroy the school in the hopes of getting an Extreme Makeover and the classroom of your dreams. _Carefully read the attached witness testimonies for your additional storylines._

Here's the tricky part: Until the detectives learn that someone suspects you, don't tip them off. They may come to you initially to get information about the fire. Just say you don't know anything about it. Don't defend yourself until you are actually accused. The detectives will be back as soon as they have a lead. _____ and _____ are character witnesses for you. They believe in you! Mention their names to the detectives if you need someone to help defend you.

© Prufrock Press Inc. • _Crime Scene Detective: Arson_
This page may be photocopied or reproduced with permission for student use.

Witnesses Who Suspect _____ (Suspect 5)

Witness 5A: _____

Witness 5B: _____

Witness 5C: _____

You are among several staff members (those listed above) who believe
_____ (Suspect 5) may have been responsible for the
fire. You think she started the fire in hopes of getting the school an Extreme
Makeover. Here is some information about _____ (Suspect
5).

_____ (Suspect 5) really enjoys teaching but has always
been frustrated with the layout and design of her classroom. She is sure that
the architect paid more attention to the cost factor instead of the kid factor and
thinks all of the classrooms are too small. She is constantly describing what her
ideal classroom would look like.

_____ (Suspect 5) thinks the library is even worse. She
says it is difficult to take a class to use the library without students falling all
over each other. There is no room to spread out when doing research and
storage space for teacher resources is scarce. Books, technology, and other
equipment are shoved into every nook and cranny, making them difficult to
find and check out.

You know _____ (Suspect 5) is a big fan of the TV show
"Extreme Makeover: Home Edition" and thinks that it is just wonderful what
Ty and his design team do to help others. You've heard all about last week's
episode on a family who lost everything due to a terrible fire. The next thing
you know, _____ (Suspect 5) is talking about "Extreme
Makeover: School Edition." That whole concept is a little extreme to you.

You believe _____ (Suspect 5) may have started the fire
so that the school could be rebuilt with the help of Ty and his design team.

When the detectives interview you, share your concerns with them. *Be sure
to mention your unique observations as listed on the next page.* You may also share
the names of the others on the above list to support your theory. Feel free to
read directly off your paper if you need to, to ensure that the information is
given accurately.

If you don't know how to answer a question, you can always say, "I
just don't know," or "I don't remember," or make up something *reasonable.*
Sometimes people who know the same person will give conflicting reports
about that person. Sorting through all of the testimony is just part of the
detective's job. Just remember that you suspect _____
(Suspect 5) was involved in the fire and your answers and statements should
reflect that suspicion.

Special Notes for Witnesses Who Suspect

_____ (Suspect 5)

Witness 5A:

Your classroom is right next to _____'s (Suspect 5) classroom. You have often had discussions about the difficulty of fitting so many students into your rooms. By the time you get all of the desks in, there is barely enough room to walk around, let alone have any kind of independent study areas. _____'s (Suspect 5) room is even smaller than yours. During a conversation you had last week, _____ (Suspect 5) said she was desperately trying to think of creative ways to get more useable space in her classroom. She always watches "Extreme Makeover: Home Edition" and was talking about how creative Ty and his design team were. She mentioned last week's story about the family whose house burned down. She said, *"Ty needs to do an 'Extreme Makeover: School Edition' and I think our school should be the first episode. Maybe we can arrange for a fire to happen at our school."* Be sure to share that quote with the detectives. You thought she was joking about arranging a fire but when you heard about the fire in the library, you immediately thought of _____ (Suspect 5). After all, her classroom is very close to the library, so a fire in the library could have easily spread to her classroom.

Witness 5B:

You eat lunch with _____ (Suspect 5) and your topic of discussion last week was the crowded library situation. You both struggle when it comes to taking your class to the library. There simply is not enough space. You also think the physical arrangement of the library is not conducive to learning or working. When you discussed ways to improve the library, _____ (Suspect 5) jokingly said, *"Only an Extreme Makeover can save our school. I think a fire would definitely improve the library. We just need to burn it down and start over."* Be sure to share that quote with the detectives. When you heard about the fire, you immediately thought of _____ (Suspect 5) and her plan to get a new library. _____ (Witness 5C) was in the lunch room with you and can confirm this story.

Witness 5C:

You eat lunch with _____ (Suspect 5) and _____ (Witness 5B). You overheard the entire "we need a new library, get rid of the old one" story (see Witness 5B's story line above). You thought _____ (Suspect 5) was just joking, but when you ran into her in the hall later, she started talking about it again. _____ (Suspect 5) said, *"I think I'll contact the producers of Extreme Makeover to see if they have ever considered taking on a school as a worthy cause."* Be sure to share that with the detectives. When you found out about the fire, you immediately thought of _____ (Suspect 5) and wondered if she would get her Extreme Makeover after all.

© Prufrock Press Inc. • *Crime Scene Detective: Arson*
This page may be photocopied or reproduced with permission for student use.

Character Witnesses for _____ (Suspect 5)

Witness 5A:

Witness 5B:

Several staff members suspect _____ (Suspect 5) was involved in some way in the fire. You are a character witness for her. You know nothing about the fire or the crime scene. If a detective questions you about the crime scene itself, you know that the fire was in the library and that's it.

Here's the tricky part: When you are first interviewed by detectives, they may not suspect _____ (Suspect 5), so don't defend her character until the detectives ask you specifically about her.

When the detectives ask you about _____ (Suspect 5), please elaborate in your own words, making up things about her that would lead the police to believe she is a wonderful person who would do no wrong (e.g., you have known her for years; you know she could never do anything like this; every time you see her she is so nice—she always has a kind word to say; she has told you how much she enjoys working here; she is so dedicated; and so on).

If you don't know how to answer a question, you can always say, "I just don't know" or "I don't remember." Sometimes people who know the same person will give conflicting reports about that person. Sorting through all of the testimony is just part of the detective's job. Just remember you are in _____'s (Suspect 5) corner.

Special Notes for Character Witnesses for _____ (Suspect 5)

Character Witness 5A:

You left school at 3:30 p.m. on the day of the fire. As you were leaving, you saw _____ (Suspect 5) in her car pulling out of the parking lot. Be sure to mention this exact time to the detectives. You might just be the alibi she needs.

Suspect 6 Profile

Suspect 6: _____

Your Story

You are a big Dr. Phil fan. You enjoy watching his show and record it every day. You've read several of the books he has authored. You think he has so much common sense wisdom to share, and you love how he tells it like it is. For 2 years now, you have tried to get tickets to be in the audience of his show, but have been unsuccessful in your attempt. You would do anything to meet Dr. Phil. You are even looking for ways to be a guest on the show.

You visit his Web site daily and are always checking out the "Be on the Show" link. One topic in particular catches your eye: "People who put themselves at risk to save others." You are always thinking of other people, so you are sure you can find some way to "save" someone else. This might be the break you are waiting for!

On the day of the fire, you stayed late after school to plan your next amazing lesson. You were going to go to the library to look for resources. As you were walking to the library (about 3:50 p.m.), you smelled smoke. You went to the library and saw the flames. You saw that the smoke was thick and black. The flames were *"orangish"* or *yellow* in color. *This information will be vital to the investigation so make sure you don't change these colors.*

You ran back to your classroom and called 911. You were at the library as the firefighters entered the building. You tried to help, but were soon escorted out of the building.

When questioned, emphasize the fact that because of *you* the fire was contained to the library and did a minimal amount of damage. It is important that you "build yourself up" and make sure the detectives know that you believe you put yourself at risk to save others in the building. You can even mention the word *hero* if you like! Stress how helpful you were to the firefighters.

Several staff members in the building believe you could have started the fire in the library to draw attention to yourself. *Carefully read the attached witness testimonies for your additional storylines.*

Here's the tricky part: Until the detectives learn that someone suspects you, don't tip them off. They may come to you initially to get information about the fire. Just tell them what you know about the color of the flame and smoke. Don't defend yourself until you are actually accused. The detectives will be back as soon as they have a lead.

_____ and _____ will be character witnesses for you. They believe in you! Mention their names to the detectives if you need someone to help defend you.

© Prufrock Press Inc. • *Crime Scene Detective: Arson*
This page may be photocopied or reproduced with permission for student use.

Witnesses Who Suspect _____ (Suspect 6)

Witness 6A: _____

Witness 6B: _____

Witness 6C: _____

You are among several staff members (those listed above) who believe
_____ (Suspect 6) may have been responsible for the fire.
You think she started and then reported the fire to draw attention to herself.
Here is some information about _____ (Suspect 6).

_____ (Suspect 6) is a big Dr. Phil fan. She enjoys
watching his show and records it every day. She has read several of the books
Dr. Phil has authored. _____ (Suspect 6) thinks he has so
much common sense wisdom to share. For 2 years now, she has tried to get
tickets to be in the audience of his show, but has been unsuccessful in her
attempt. _____ (Suspect 6) would do anything to meet Dr.
Phil and is even looking for ways to be a guest on the show.

_____ (Suspect 6) visits the Dr. Phil Web site daily and
is always checking out the "Be on the Show" link. One topic in particular has
caught her eye: "People who put themselves at risk to save others."

When the detectives
interview you, share your
concerns with them. *Be sure to
mention your unique observations
as listed on the next page.* You
may also share the names of
the others on the above list
to support your theory. Feel
free to read directly off your
paper if you need to, to ensure
that the information is given
accurately.

If you don't know how to
answer a question, you can
always say, "I just don't know,"
or "I don't remember," or
make up something *reasonable*.
Sometimes people who know
the same person will give
conflicting reports about that
person. Sorting through all of
the testimony is just part of the
detective's job. Just remember
that you suspect _____
_____ (Suspect 6) was
involved in the fire and your
answers and statements should
reflect that suspicion.

© Prufrock Press Inc. • *Crime Scene Detective: Arson*
This page may be photocopied or reproduced with permission for student use.

Special Notes for Witnesses Who Suspect

_____ (Suspect 6)

Witness 6A:

Because you and _____ (Suspect 6) are on the same teaching team, you spend lots of time together throughout the year. You know that she is a huge Dr. Phil fan. She is always talking about his talk show. When there are any conflicts at faculty or team meetings, she always gives advice starting with "Dr. Phil says that . . . ." She is constantly talking about ways to get on the show. She is really upset that after trying for 2 years she still has not gotten tickets to be in the audience.

At one of your meetings last week, _____ (Suspect 6) was talking about how a proposed topic for an upcoming Dr. Phil show was "People who put themselves at risk to save other people." She said that this might just be her lucky break. When you questioned what she had done to save other people she said, *"Oh, nothing yet, but life is all about taking risks, and I'm prepared to do whatever I need to do to save people."* Be sure to share that quote with the detectives. When you hear _____ (Suspect 6) was the one who reported the fire and claims she saved many lives, you thought immediately of her desire to get on Dr. Phil. It just seemed suspicious to you.

Witness 6B:

On Thursday after the fire, you were talking to _____ (Suspect 6). She made it very clear that she was the one who spotted the fire and called 911. She kept going on and on about *"saving so many lives"* and even went as far as calling herself a *"hero."* She was looking for the daily newspaper to see if her picture was in it along with the story about the fire. You thought it was odd that she was bragging so much. It's like she was trying to get everyone to put her on a pedestal for "saving" the school from burning down. She even said, *"I've already written up my heroic, life-saving actions and will be contacting Dr. Phil today. I just know he will be calling me now. Surely this is Dr. Phil-worthy!"* You thought that was very strange. Although she laughed when she said it, her body language suggested she was serious. Be sure to share her statement with the detectives.

Witness 6C:

On Thursday morning, the first day back after the fire, _____ (Suspect 6) walked into the office where you were. She made it very clear that she was the one who spotted the fire and called 911. She kept going on and on about *"risking her life to save the lives of others"* and even went as far as calling herself a *"hero."* She was looking for the daily newspaper to see if her picture was in it along with the story of the fire. You thought it was odd that she was bragging so much. It's like she was trying to get everyone to put her on a pedestal for "saving" the school from burning down. The oddest thing of all, however, was when *she asked your opinion for what she should wear when she appears on the Dr. Phil show.* She feels confident that Dr. Phil will be inviting her to be a guest on the show featuring "people who risk their lives to save others." Be sure to share her comments with the detectives.

© Prufrock Press Inc. • *Crime Scene Detective: Arson*
This page may be photocopied or reproduced with permission for student use.

Character Witnesses for _____ (Suspect 6)

Character Witness 6A: _____

Character Witness 6B: _____

Several staff members suspect _____ (Suspect 6) was involved in some way in the fire. You are a character witness for her. You know nothing about the fire or the crime scene. If a detective questions you about the crime scene itself, you know that the fire was in the library and that's it.

Here's the tricky part: When you are first interviewed by the detectives, they may not suspect _____ (Suspect 6), so don't defend her character until the detectives ask you specifically about her.

When the detectives ask you about _____ (Suspect 6), please elaborate in your own words, making up things about her that would lead the detectives to believe she is a wonderful person who would do no wrong (e.g., you have known her for years; you know she could never do anything like this; every time you see her she is so nice—she always has a kind word to say; she has told you how much she enjoys working here; she is such a conscientious person; she is so dedicated; and so on).

If you don't know how to answer a question, you can always say, "I just don't know" or "I don't remember." Sometimes people who know the same person will give conflicting reports about that person. Sorting through all of the testimony is just part of the detective's job. Just remember, you are in _____ 's (Suspect 6) corner.

Special Notes for Character Witnesses for_____ (Suspect 6)

Character Witness 6A: _____

On the day of the fire, you were heading out of the building around 3:20 p.m. to go home. You saw _____ (Suspect 6) in her classroom and stopped to chat for a few minutes. You aren't sure of the exact time but you think you probably left her classroom and the school around 3:40 p.m. Be sure to give the detectives these exact times as you may just be the alibi _____ (Suspect 6) needs.

Character Witness 6B: _____

You also watch Dr. Phil everyday. You and _____ (Suspect 6) will often spend time before school talking about the previous day's show. You are hoping to get tickets to see a taping of his show this coming summer. You don't think _____ (Suspect 6) would ever be so desperate as to start a fire to get on Dr. Phil.

© Prufrock Press Inc. • Crime Scene Detective: Arson
This page may be photocopied or reproduced with permission for student use.

Student Sheet: Detective Report

It is the policy of this Police Department to do weekly debriefings. Each detective will provide a written summary of his or her activity for the week. Please include the following information in your typed report.

1. Describe what you saw at the crime scene and give your interpretation of the evidence found there. Be specific. (Do this for your first report only.)

2. Tell who you have questioned and describe what information you received from that person. Analyze what it may mean for the case.

3. Tell you who suspect so far and why.

4. Include a recommendation as to how the department should proceed with the case.

© Prufrock Press Inc. • *Crime Scene Detective: Arson*
This page may be photocopied or reproduced with permission for student use.

Evidence Request Card

Name of detective:_____ Date of request: _____

Name of suspect:_____

Type of evidence requested:_____

_____

Reasons to support request of evidence from the above-named suspect:_____

_____

Request granted ❏   Request denied ❏

Comments:_____

_____

Sergeant's signature:_____   Lab technician's signature:_____

Evidence Request Card

Name of detective:_____ Date of request: _____

Name of suspect:_____

Type of evidence requested:_____

_____

Reasons to support request of evidence from the above-named suspect:_____

_____

Request granted ❏   Request denied ❏

Comments:_____

_____

Sergeant's signature:_____   Lab technician's signature:_____

Forensic Lab Evidence Log

Staple several copies of this form to the inside of the folder for each type of evidence.
Use this form to record when the evidence has been given to a detective and when the evidence is returned.

Date	Detective's Name	Evidence Viewed	Time In	Time Out

© Prufrock Press Inc. • *Crime Scene Detective: Arson*
This page may be photocopied or reproduced with permission for student use.

Procedures for Crime Lab Technician

Blood Evidence

Students will be coming to you to get the results of evidence obtained at the fire. The evidence folder will contain a general statement summarizing information about the blood found at the scene. Your job is to share the contents of the folder with the students and to give them blood types of likely suspects. Do not give students the folder, because the blood types of all of the suspects will be listed on the same page.

Detectives will have an Evidence Request Card signed by the sergeant (teacher), naming the individual for whom they would like to have the blood type. Only share with students the blood type of the suspect indicated on their Evidence Request Card. Don't tell them the blood types of all the suspects. Students may not realize a certain individual is a suspect.

When a detective comes to your lab, please follow these procedures:

1. Ask to see the Evidence Request Card signed by the sergeant. If the student does not have a card, you should not, *under any circumstances*, let him or her see the evidence.
2. After verifying the card, initial it, return it to the detective, and then have him or her sign in on the evidence log.
3. *Read* the general report in the evidence folder to the detective.
4. Along with this report, provide him or her with the blood type of the designated suspect. Give out only the blood type of the suspect that has been approved on the Evidence Request Card.
5. Have the detective sign out to indicate that the evidence was received verbally.
6. Do not allow students to view the entire evidence folder or remove evidence from the lab.

Procedures for Crime Lab Technician

All Evidence Except Blood

Students will be coming to you to get the results of evidence obtained at the fire. The evidence folder will contain general statements summarizing information about the evidence found at the crime scene (fingerprints, shoe prints, hair, handwriting, or the arson report). For most labs, it will also contain a sample that was collected from the crime scene.

Your job is to share the contents of the folder with the students and to give them samples taken from likely suspects. You will keep the samples from the various suspects in a different location than the evidence that was taken from the crime scene.

Detectives will have an Evidence Request Card signed by the sergeant (teacher), naming the individual for whom they would like to see samples. They will present this card to you when they request the evidence. Only share with students the samples of the suspect indicated on the Evidence Request Card. Don't show them all of the samples. Students may not realize a certain individual is a suspect.

When a detective comes to your lab, please follow these procedures:
1. Ask to see the Evidence Request Card signed by the sergeant. If the student does not have a card, you should not, *under any circumstances*, let him or her see the evidence.
2. After verifying the card, initial it, return it to the detective, and then have him or her sign in on the evidence log.
3. Show the detective the evidence folder containing the report and the evidence (fingerprints, shoe prints, hair, handwriting, etc.) that was taken from the crime scene. In addition, provide him or her with the sample from the designated suspect only.
4. Have the detective sign out to indicate that the evidence was returned. Double check to make sure all evidence is returned.
5. Do not allow students to view the entire evidence folder or remove evidence from the lab.

© Prufrock Press Inc. • *Crime Scene Detective: Arson*
This page may be photocopied or reproduced with permission for student use.

Official Report: Blood Evidence

This report is to remain in the possession of the lab technician at all times.

Read the general report to the detectives who request information about the suspected blood found at the scene of the crime.

General Report

Lab results show that a red substance found on a tissue at the scene of the crime is indeed blood. This tissue containing the blood was found on the floor next to the computers that were damaged in the fire.

Further analysis shows the blood type left at the scene of the fire to be **type A.**

Give detectives the blood type of just the suspect approved on the Evidence Request Card.

Suspects' Blood Types

_____(Suspect 1)   A

_____(Suspect 2)   A

_____(Suspect 3)   A

_____(Suspect 4)   O

_____(Suspect 5)   O

_____(Suspect 6)   O

Make sure these blood types agree with the ones on each suspect's identification card. If different types are given on the cards, change this listing accordingly.

Official Seal · Office of Forensic Sciences

Official Report: Arson Lab

The fire department received a call from
_____ School at approximately 3:50
p.m. The caller, _____, reported a
fire in the library media center. An emergency truck
and firefighters arrived at approximately 4 p.m.

Upon arriving at the scene, firefighters reported
seeing thick black smoke and a flame that was
orangish-yellow in color.

The fire was contained to the library media center
and was promptly put out. No one was injured as a
result of the fire.

Arson Investigator Matthew Taylor and an
accelerant detection canine, Blaze, examined the
area immediately after the fire was extinguished.
Accelerants were detected in multiple areas in the
room. It has been determined that books soaked in a
chemical were used to start the fire. The results of
the chemical analysis tests are pending.

Piles of these books were found on the floor in
front of the copy machine and on the floor next to a
video storage shelf in the video storage closet. A
wooden structure in the fire had burned approximately
3/4 of an inch. Small cracks were found in the glass
on the copy machine.

Note for Teachers:

Write the name of suspect 6 in the space for the caller.
Cover up this note before placing the report in the evidence folder.
Students should not know that this person is a suspect.

© Prufrock Press Inc. • *Crime Scene Detective: Arson*
This page may be photocopied or reproduced with permission for student use.

Official Report: Fingerprint Evidence

Three fingerprints were located on the door leading into the library media center. These were the only prints found that could be recovered. The three prints are shown below.

Official Report: Shoe Print Evidence

Two shoe prints were found at the scene. One print was located near the door leading into the library media center. A second print was on the floor in front of the metal storage shelf located in the library media center.

The prints were identical. One of the prints recovered from the scene is shown on the attached page.

© Prufrock Press Inc. • *Crime Scene Detective: Arson*
This page may be photocopied or reproduced with permission for student use.

Official Report: Hair Evidence

Several strands of hair were found in the library media center. They were found on a metal shelving unit that contains videos. This shelving unit is located on the back wall of the storage room.

The hair samples were collected and placed on the attached index card.

Official Report: Handwriting Evidence

A list was found on the floor in the storage room. The list consisted of the following words: lighter fluid, matches, kerosene, fire extinguisher, milk, and bread.

The list was taken into evidence and is attached.

© Prufrock Press Inc. • *Crime Scene Detective: Arson*
This page may be photocopied or reproduced with permission for student use.

Appendix A:
Instructions for Creating Your Own Simulation

Getting Started

This section gives guidelines for writing and staging your own crime scene simulation. The simulation can be as detailed and in-depth as you choose it to be. It can have as little as 3 pieces of evidence or more than 10 pieces of evidence. You may have 10 people involved or your entire school staff. The location will depend on your crime.

You will be creating your own crime story, but you can use the supporting materials such as the forensic lab procedures, evidence log, and suspect identification cards provided in the given simulation rather than creating your own forms.

Getting Participants

You will first need to ask staff members to play the roles of suspects, witnesses, and lab technicians. Ask for volunteers from your faculty and staff to play the various roles. Your crime scene storylines will depend on how many volunteers you get to participate. Based on this number, determine how many suspects you will have. Each suspect should have at least three people with collaborating stories pointing to the guilt of the suspect. Each suspect should also have at least two people to serve as character witnesses, claiming the suspect must certainly be innocent of the crime or who can provide an alibi.

Extra volunteers can serve as people who witness the fire, red herrings, or lab technicians who handle the physical evidence. Choose participants from all grade levels and include the secretarial and administrative staff. This broad base of participants will require students to interview almost everyone in the school in order to get enough clues to solve the crime.

Choosing a Crime

One of the first things you will have to do is decide on a crime. It should be a crime that could take place in your school and one that involves staff members. Arson makes a great crime to simulate because there are seven possible motives to work with. See Appendix B for a description of the motives. Avoid using a murder for a crime. It may generate motives and discussions not appropriate for a school environment.

Writing the Story

Now that you've chosen your crime and have selected volunteers, begin creating your storylines. Start by writing a motive for each suspect. After you have established a motive and a reason for being at the crime scene for each suspect, select several witnesses who think the person is guilty. Come up with a connection between the suspect and those witnesses who suspect him or her (common planning time, department meeting, on the same team, or carpool together) to link them together. Do the same for the character witnesses. The goal is to write a story that establishes both a motive and an opportunity for the suspect to have committed the crime. Ideally, each storyline will convince the students that the suspect is guilty. They will need to use the evidence left at the crime scene to determine the guilt or innocence of a person.

Deciding on Evidence

Determine what evidence would be left at the scene of the crime. Consider using handwriting, hair, fiber from clothing, fingerprints, footprints, or simulated blood. Choose things that could actually be left at a crime scene and that would be unique to each suspect. Make a form to request this information from the suspects or use the one provided on pp. 47–48.

Article Describing the Event

Write a newspaper article that will introduce students and faculty volunteers to the crime. You may also use the one provided on p. 44.

Preparing Materials

After writing the following materials, duplicate them and give them to the appropriate people:
- Give each witness a:
  - newspaper article,
  - witness role description sheet, and
  - witness information sheet (this contains the storylines for all witnesses who suspect a given suspect).
- Give each suspect and the guilty person a:
  - newspaper article,
  - suspect role description sheet,
  - suspect profile sheet (different for each person),
  - witness information sheet for each specific suspect (this contains the storylines for all witnesses who suspect a given suspect), and
  - request for evidence samples.

Getting Evidence

Prior to setting up the crime scene, gather evidence from all identified suspects. When you hand out suspect storylines to the people designated as suspects, give them an evidence request sheet detailing the evidence that you need.

Ask each suspect to complete a Suspect Identification Card (use p. 49). Take a picture with a digital camera and include it on the card.

Setting up the Labs

The number of labs you establish will depend on the number of volunteers you have. You may keep all of the evidence in one location or in a couple of rooms. It is best to have at least two different locations so more students can view evidence at the same time with less congestion. For example, the students may view fingerprints and footprints in the same lab but go to another location to view handwriting and hair samples. Post a sign outside the door identifying the location as a forensic lab.

Your simulation may use a variety of evidence such as blood, handwriting, hair, shoe prints, and fingerprints. Although the evidence may all be viewed in the same lab, you will need to set up a separate file for each type of evidence.

On the outside of a file folder write the type of evidence (fingerprints, shoe prints, etc.). In the folder place the official report for that specific piece of evidence and any physical evidence recovered from the crime scene. Keep all the suspects' evidence samples in separate envelopes, using a different envelope for each type of evidence. Label each file folder with the type of evidence it contains. For example, the file folder labeled "Fingerprints" will contain all of the suspects' fingerprint samples in separate envelopes. This file folder and its contents will always remain in the possession of the lab technician. By organizing evidence this way, the lab technician can hand the students the information recovered from the crime scene without showing them all of the suspects' evidence samples. At the time they visit the lab, detectives may not know who all of the suspects are, so you don't want them to see all of the suspects' evidence. The lab technician will just give the students the evidence sample from the suspect they've requested.

After arriving at the lab, students will need to fill in the Forensic Lab Evidence Log (see p. 80) Make several copies of the log sheet and staple them to the inside of a folder. You should have one folder per lab. This log documents that the students have handled the evidence in question. If you have more than one class doing the simulation at the same time, you may have a different folder for each class to ensure confidentiality during the investigation. Give the lab technician a copy of the procedures for viewing evidence (see pp. 81–82). *Note*: A magnifying glass or microscope located at the lab is helpful for students viewing the trace evidence.

Set up the Crime Scene

Choose an area in the school that would be appropriate for your storylines. This should be an area that is easily accessible to all suspects. Check with your local police department for crime scene tape to section off the crime scene or use another type of brightly colored tape.

Decide what types of evidence would fit with your crime. Suggestions for creating and placing evidence can be found on pp. 38–39. Place the evidence you have selected at appropriate places at the scene.

Remember, all of this evidence is circumstantial. Students will have to tie in witness statements, establish a motive, and build a strong case to prove the suspect guilty.

Viewing the Crime Scene

Let teachers and staff know that the investigation has begun. They can review their statements and be prepared for an interview. Before taking students to the crime scene, distribute the newspaper article concerning the alleged crime. You can fill in the empty spaces on p. 44 or you can write an article that is more specific to your school. Read and discuss the article. Ask students to predict what types of evidence they may see or what they may be looking for. Review the police procedures at a crime scene information on p. 10.

Take students to the crime scene. Have them first sketch the room. After completing this, they may look around the room without touching anything. You don't want to destroy any evidence. When sketching the room, students should record the pieces of possible evidence they have found. Give everyone a significant amount of time to view the scene.

Discuss the evidence discovered, reviewing the difference between circumstantial and direct evidence. Ask for student volunteers to mark each piece of evidence with some sort of indicator such as an orange cone. You can easily make cones out of construction paper. At this time, you could also have them take measurements from each piece of evidence to two different fixed objects in the room. Take pictures of the crime scene with a digital camera. If you have access to a computer, place these pictures into a file in the computer or print them out so that students can always have access to the crime scene even after you take it down.

Use any remaining class time to generate ideas of who may have committed the crime, to discuss possible motives (remember the seven motives for starting a fire), and to develop a plan of action for proceeding with the investigation.

Student Procedures

If you have more than one class working on the case, make each class a different police precinct. A competition between the classes to see who can solve the case first adds to the excitement. Be sure to keep the investigation of each class confidential.

Students should not be told which faculty members are participating. Just like in real life, a list of suspects isn't left behind at the crime scene. After visiting the crime scene, students may want to read through the news article again. This article will give the students a few ideas of where to begin. Usually students will begin interviewing people they know well. Sometimes they will get a lead that pays off, sometimes they won't.

As a class, decide which students will interview which staff members. Students should work in pairs to make sure all information from the interview gets noted. Students should always be prepared for an interview by taking with them a list of predetermined questions and paper and pen to record answers.

Questioning Procedures

Interviewing faculty and staff members is a difficult skill. Be sure to spend time discussing the types of questions that will get desired answers. Students should avoid asking "yes" or "no" questions. A student should not ask, "Did you start the fire?" because a guilty person would naturally answer the question with a "no." Instead, students should ask questions like, "Where were you on the day or time of the fire?", "Do you know anyone who might have a motive for doing this?", and "Have you noticed anyone behaving suspiciously or out of character?" A favorite follow-up question is, "What's the worst thing that will happen to you if you tell the truth?" Sometimes you can catch a person off guard with that question. As a class, brainstorm a list of questions that would be appropriate to ask. Narrow this list down to a maximum of 10 questions, ordering them in an appropriate manner. Have the students write down these questions for future reference. Additional questions not on the original list may need to be asked while the investigation is underway.

It will be beneficial to the students to practice interviewing each other before interviewing teachers and staff members. Encourage the students to ask follow up questions as new information becomes available during the interview. Be sure students each have paper for recording statements. Remind the students that they should be polite and considerate of those they are interviewing at all times.

Students should set up times to interview staff members before or after school, during lunch, or during planning time. Before interviewing anyone, students should identify themselves as a detective from your classroom.

Examining Evidence at the Lab

When, in your opinion, students have interviewed enough people and have a sufficient amount of evidence pointing to a suspect, you may let them complete an Evidence Request Card (see p. 79) that allows them to go to the designated forensic labs to see the physical evidence. Students must have established probable cause to view evidence at the forensic lab. In real life, police don't have records on every person in the world. The same is true here. Students can't just ask to see fingerprints and hair samples from every teacher in the school.

On the request cards, student detectives must list the type of evidence they are requesting, the suspect they are requesting it for, and justify why that person is a suspect. Only with teacher approval can they proceed to the lab. Once approved, they go to the lab, give the card to the lab technician, and then view the evidence. They may only see the evidence found at the crime scene and the evidence of the suspect that has been approved. After visiting the lab, students report their findings back to the class. When visiting a lab, it is best to send the students in smaller groups or with a partner. The number you send at one time will depend on the size and location of your lab. It generally does not work well to send the entire class at the same time.

Charging a Suspect

Students may charge a suspect with the crime when they have interviewed the majority of the key witnesses, gathered enough information, and have sufficient physical evidence. If you are not going to have a mock trial, then you may tell the students if they are right at this point in the simulation. You could also have students present the case to you as if they were prosecuting attorneys. This could be a written statement or oral presentation.

If you are going to hold a mock trial, do not tell the students if they charged the right person. It will be up to the mock trial jury to decide the guilt or innocence of the charged. After the jury has made its decision you may reveal the name of the guilty person.

Appendix B: Arson Motives

1. Vanity

A person starts a fire because he or she wants to be the hero, save people, or get public recognition.

2. Crime Concealment

Using a fire to hide a theft or other crime can be a motive.

3. Juvenile

Fires are started by kids under the age of 16 who do it just for fun.

4. Insurance Fraud

People can start a fire for financial gain or to offset the losses from a failing business.

5. Pyromaniac

A pyromaniac is a person who enjoys setting fires and gets a thrill out of seeing things burn.

6. Civil Disorder

When people are protesting certain conditions, their actions sometimes result in burning down a church, government office, or an abortion clinic.

7. Spite or Revenge

When someone is very angry, he or she may burn down someone's house or business to get revenge.

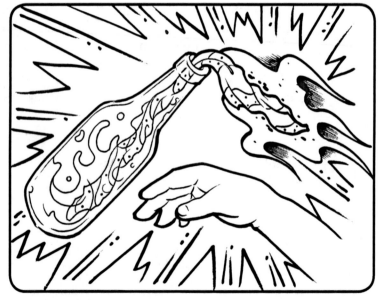

© Prufrock Press Inc. • *Crime Scene Detective: Arson*
This page may be photocopied or reproduced with permission for student use.

Appendix C: Fast Facts on Fires

Temperature

- 1200° F—temperature at which aluminum melts
- 1550° F—temperature at which a normal house fire burns
- 1981° F—temperature at which copper melts
- 2781° F—temperature at which steel melts

Conclusions

- In a typical (accidental) house fire, you would expect anything aluminum to melt.
- If copper and steel melt, an accelerant was used.

Other Indicators

- Small cracks (crazing) on glass indicate a fast, hot fire, which means an accelerant was used to start the fire.
- Large cracks on glass indicate a slow fire, which means an accelerant was not used.
- Wood burns at 1 inch per 45 minutes.

Color of Flame as it Relates to Temperature of Fire

Flame Color	Temperature (F)
Faint red	900°
Blood red	1050°
Bright red	1550°
Orange	1725°
Lemon	1825°
White	2200°
Blue white	2250°

Color of Smoke Created by Certain Combustibles

Smoke Color	Combustible
White	Phosphorous
White to gray	Benzine
Yellow to brownish yellow	Sulfur, sulfuric acid, gunpowder
Greenish yellow	Chlorine gas
Gray to brown	Wood, paper, cloth
Violet	Iodine
Brown	Cooking oil
Brownish black	Lacquer thinner
Black to brown	Turpentine
Black	Acetone, kerosene, gasoline, lubricating oil, rubber, tar, coal, foamed plastics

Appendix D: Resources

Books

Cook, N. (1995). *Classifying fingerprints.* Parsippany, NJ: Dale Seymour Publications.

Jackson, D. (1996). *The bone detectives: How forensic anthropologists solve crimes and uncover mysteries of the dead.* Boston: Little, Brown & Company.

Owen, D. (2002). *Police lab: How forensic science tracks down and convicts criminals.* Buffalo, NY: Firefly Books Ltd.

Platt, R. (2005). *Crime scene: The ultimate guide to forensic science.* New York: Dorling Kindersley.

Platt, R. (2005). *Forensics.* Boston: Kingfisher Knowledge.

Sheely, R. (1993). *Police lab: Using science to solve crimes.* New York: Silver Moon Press.

Thomas, P. (1995). *Talking bones: The science of forensic anthropology.* New York: Facts On File.

Forensic Science Kits and Materials

Carolina Biological Supply Company
1-800-334-5551
http://www.carolina.com

Ward's Natural Science
1-800-962-2660
http://www.wardsci.com

Note: Both Carolina Biological Supply Company and Ward's have a variety of forensic science activity kits including fingerprinting, document analysis, hair analysis, and fiber identification. These are helpful in conducting science experiments and activities during this unit. They also have additional resources such as fingerprint powder, simulated blood and bones, and ballistic models to enhance students' understanding of various forensic topics.

Answer Key

The Field of Forensic Science Quiz

I. Matching

1. B
2. G
3. J
4. E
5. H
6. I
7. C
8. D
9. A
10. F

II. Sequence of Events

Police procedures at a crime scene

A. 5
B. 3
C. 2
D. 1
E. 4

Using scientific method in an investigation

A. 5
B. 1
C. 4
D. 3
E. 2

III. Fill in the Blank

1. Forensic science
2. Locard's principle
3. direct
4. circumstantial

About the Author

Karen Schulz received her bachelor's degree in elementary education and mathematics from Southern Illinois University at Carbondale in 1984. She received a master's degree in teaching from Webster University in 1989. In 1996, she earned her gifted certification from Webster University. She currently teaches at Wildwood Middle School in the Rockwood School District. Karen has been teaching middle school gifted education since 1993. Prior to teaching gifted education she taught mathematics.

Over the years, Karen has presented her forensic curriculum at numerous gifted education conferences. In 2001, Karen received the national Education's Unsung Hero Award from ING Northern Annuity for her work in developing a forensic science curriculum for her classroom. In the fall of 2005, she won a national competition sponsored by Olympus America and Tool Factory, for her continuing work with forensics in the classroom.

Karen creates much of her own curriculum. Recognizing that there was a lack of quality materials available in the area of forensics, Karen developed the simulation and storylines that eventually were published as *Crime Scene Detective*, her first book. *Crime Scene Detective: Arson* is her second book in the field of forensic applications for the gifted classroom.

Karen lives in Ballwin, MO, with her husband Jim, their daughter Taylor, and their son Matthew.

CPSIA information can be obtained
at www.ICGtesting.com
Printed in the USA
LVOW09s0128250817

546314LV00017B/855/P